A Book Of

ADVANCED C PROGRAMMING

For B.C.A.(Science) : Semester - II

[Course Code 122 : Credit - 4]

CBCS Pattern

As Per New Syllabus, Effective from June 2019

Mrs. Deepali N. Bhoskar
M. Phil, M.Sc. (Computer Application)
Visiting Lecturer at B.V.D.U.Y.M College, Pune

Mr. Kamil Ajmal Khan
Assistant Professor
B.C.A./M.C.A. Department
Abeda Inamadar Senior College, Camp, Pune

N5112

Advanced C Programming   **ISBN 978-93-89533-71-2**

First Edition	:	November 2019
©	:	Authors

Published By :
NIRALI PRAKASHAN
Abhyudaya Pragati, 1312, Shivaji Nagar,
Off J.M. Road, Pune – 411005
Tel - (020) 25512336/37/39, Fax - (020) 25511379
Email : niralipune@pragationline.com

➢ DISTRIBUTION CENTRES

PUNE

Nirali Prakashan (For orders within Pune)	:	119, Budhwar Peth, Jogeshwari Mandir Lane, Pune 411002, Maharashtra Tel : (020) 2445 2044; Mobile : 9657703145 Email : niralilocal@pragationline.com
Nirali Prakashan (For orders outside Pune)	:	S. No. 28/27, Dhayari, Near Asian College Pune 411041 Tel : (020) 24690204; Mobile : 9657703143 Email : bookorder@pragationline.com

MUMBAI

Nirali Prakashan	:	385, S.V.P. Road, Rasdhara Co-op. Hsg. Society Ltd., Girgaum, Mumbai 400004, Maharashtra; Mobile : 9320129587 Tel : (022) 2385 6339 / 2386 9976, Fax : (022) 2386 9976 Email : niralimumbai@pragationline.com

➢ DISTRIBUTION BRANCHES

JALGAON

Nirali Prakashan	:	34, V. V. Golani Market, Navi Peth, Jalgaon 425001, Maharashtra, Tel : (0257) 222 0395, Mob : 94234 91860; Email : niralijalgaon@pragationline.com

KOLHAPUR

Nirali Prakashan	:	New Mahadvar Road, Kedar Plaza, 1st Floor Opp. IDBI Bank, Kolhapur 416 012 Maharashtra. Mob : 9850046155; Email : niralikolhapur@pragationline.com

NAGPUR

Nirali Prakashan	:	Above Maratha Mandir, Shop No. 3, First Floor, Rani Jhanshi Square, Sitabuldi, Nagpur 440012, Maharashtra Tel : (0712) 254 7129; Email : niralinagpur@pragationline.com

DELHI

Nirali Prakashan	:	4593/15, Basement, Agarwal Lane, Ansari Road, Daryaganj Near Times of India Building, New Delhi 110002 Mob : 08505972553 Email : niralidelhi@pragationline.com

BENGALURU

Nirali Prakashan	:	Maitri Ground Floor, Jaya Apartments, No. 99, 6th Cross, 6th Main, Malleswaram, Bengaluru 560003, Karnataka; Mob : 9449043034 Email: niralibangalore@pragationline.com

Other Branches : Hyderabad, Chennai

niralipune@pragationline.com | www.pragationline.com
Also find us on 🅕 www.facebook.com/niralibooks

Preface ...

We take this opportunity to present this book entitled as **"Advanced C Programming"** to the students of Second Semester - BCA (Science). The object of this book is to present the subject matter in a most concise and simple manner. The book is written strictly according to the New Syllabus.

The book has its own unique features. It brings out the subject in a very simple and lucid manner for easy and comprehensive understanding of the basic concepts, its intricacies, procedures and practices. This book will help the readers to have a broader view on Advanced C Programming. The language used in this book is easy and will help students to improve their vocabulary of Technical terms and understand the matter in a better and happier way.

We sincerely thank Shri. Dineshbhai Furia and Shri. Jignesh Furia of Nirali Prakashan, for the confidence reposed in us and giving us this opportunity to reach out to the students of management studies.

We have given our best inputs for this book. Any suggestions towards the improvement of this book and sincere comments are most welcome on niralipune@pragationline.com.

Authors

■ ■ ■

Syllabus ...

1. Preprocessor [08 Hrs]
- Concept, Format of Preprocessor Directives, File inclusion Directives (#include), Macro Substitution Directives (#define), Nested Macros, Parameterized Macros.
- Macros Versus Functions, #error / #pragma directives, Conditional Compilation (#if/#ifdef/#else/#elif/#endif), Predefined Macros (_DATE_ / _TIME_ / _FILE_ / _LINE_/ _STDC_).

2. Pointers [08 Hrs]
- Concept – Reference and Dereference, Declaration, Definition, Initialization and Use, Types of Pointers.
- Pointer Arithmetic, Multiple Indirection.
- Parameter Passing – Call By Value and Call By Reference.
- Arrays and Pointers - Pointer to Array, Array of pointers.
- Functions and Pointers - Passing Pointer to Function, Returning Pointer from Function, Function Pointer, Pointers and const.
- Dynamic Memory Management, Allocation, Resizing, Releasing, Memory Leak / Dangling Pointers.

3. Strings [08 Hrs]
- Concept, Declaration, Definition, Initialization, Format Specifiers, String Literals/ Constants and Variables – Reading and Writing from and to Console, Importance of Terminating NULL Character, Strings and Pointers.
- Array of Strings and Array of Character Pointers, User Defined Functions, Predefined Functions in string.h - strlen, strcpy, strcat, strcmp, strcmpi, strrev, strlwr, strupr, strset, strchr, strrchr, strstr, strncpy, strncat, strncmp, strncmpi, strnset, strtok, Command Line Arguments – argc and argv.

4. Structures [08 Hrs]
- Concept, Declaration, Definition, Initialization, Accessing Structure Members (.operator).
- Array of Structures, Pointers to Structures, Declaring Pointer to Structure.
- Accessing Structure Members via Pointer to Structure, Structures and Functions.
- Passing each Member of Structure as a Separate Argument, Passing Structure by Value / Address.
- Nested Structures, typedef and Structures.

5. Advanced Features [08 Hrs]
- Unions - Concept, Declaration, Definition, Accessing Union Members, Difference between Structures and Unions, Structures within Union, Union within Structures, Pointers and Unions, Nested Unions, Enumerated Data Types, Bit Fields, Concept, Need, Use, Multi-File Programs.

6. File Handling [08 Hrs]
- Concept of Streams, Need, Types of Files, Operations on Text and Binary Files, Random Access File, Library Functions for File Handling – fopen, fclose, fgetc, fseek, fgets, fputc etc.

■■■

Contents ...

■■■

1... Preprocessor

1.1 INTRODUCTION

- The C language preprocessor is a collection of special statements, called directives that are executed at the beginning of the complication process.
- Preprocessor directives are processed by a program called a preprocessor.
- Each of the preprocessor directives begin with a hash symbol(#) and do not require semicolon at the end.

1.2 CONCEPT

- C preprocessor is a unique feature of C programming language.
- C preprocessor has many tools that are not available in other high level languages.
- These tools can be used by programmer to make his program easy to write, easy to read, easy to modify, more efficient and portable.
- **Preprocessor** is a program that processes source code before it passes through the complier.
- It operates under the control of preprocessor directives or preprocessor command line.
- Preprocessor directives are placed in source program before main ( ).
- The source code is examined by preprocessor to check, if any preprocessor directive is there before source code passes through complier.
- Before source code is handed over to compiler appropriate actions as per directives in code are taken. Then and then only source code is handed over to compiler.

1.3 FORMAT OF PREPROCESSOR DIRECTIVES

- Preprocessor directives follow special format that are different from normal C program formats.
- **Rules of Preprocessor Format:** All preprocessor directives starts with #symbol in first column and they do not require semicolon at end e.g. #include, #define.
- Preprocessor directives are placed in the source program before calling the main( ) function.
- Following is list of commonly used preprocessor directives and their functions.

Preprocessor Directives and Functions

Sr. No.	Directives	Functions
1.	#define	Defines a macro substitution.
2.	#include	Specifies files to be included.
3.	#undef	Undefines a macro.
4.	#ifdef	Test for macro definition.
5.	#endif	Specifies the end of #if.
6.	#ifndef	Tests whether a macro is not defined.
7.	#if	Test a compile time condition.
8.	#else	Specifies alternatives when #if test fails.

The above listed directives can be divided into three categories:
- File Inclusion directives (#include).
- Macro substitution directives (#define).
- Complier control directives.

1.4 FILE INCLUSION DIRECTIVES (#include)

- As a part of program an external file containing functions or macro definitions can be included.
- #include preprocessor directive is used to include an external file or macro.
- Following is the format of file inclusion directive.

```
#include "filename"
        or
#include<filename>
```

- Filename is the name of file containing required definitions or functions.
- include preprocessor inserts entire contents of filename into the source code of program.
- There is difference between "filename" and <filename> inclusion.
- When filename is included in double quotation mark, the search for file is first made in current directory and then in standard directories.
- When filename is without double quots, file is searched only in standard directories.
- Nesting of included files is allowed i.e. an included file can included another file but a file cannot include itself.
- If included file is not found, an error is reported and compilation is terminated.

Example:

Lets consider following 'C' programs were created and following are their names:

1. SYMBOLS.c — contains symbols definitions.
2. SHAPES.c — contains shapes related functions.
3. TEST.c — contains test functions.

We can add these definitions or functions to use in program by including them with #include preprocessor directive.

```
#include<stdio.h>
#include "SYMBOLS.c"
#include "SHAPES.c"
#include "TEST.c"
#define x 100
main ()
{
    ..............
    ..............
}
```

1.5 MACRO SUBSTITUTION DIRECTIVES (#define)

- An identifier in a program is replaced by a predefined string composed of one or more tokens, is called as macro substitution.
- Macro substitution process is accomplished with the help of #define directive statement.
- Macro statement is usually known as macro definition or a macro.
- Following is the format to declare a macro,
    #define identifier string
- If a macro is included in a program at the beginning, preprocessor replaces each occurrence of identifier in the source code by the string.
- #define key word is written in the first column followed by identifier and a string with at least one blank space between them.
- Note: Definition is never terminated by a semicolon.
- String may be any text whereas identifier must be a valid 'C' name.
  e.g. #define COUNT 100
- Following are common forms of macro substitution:
  1. Nested macro substitution.
  2. Parameterized macro (Argumented macro substitution).
  3. Macros Vs Functions.

Simple Macro Substitution:

- To define constants simple string replacement is used.

```
e.g.    #define      M           500
        #define      TRUE        1
        #define      SUBJECTS    4
        #define      PI          3.142
        #define      STATE       "MAHARASHTRA"
```

- All macros (Identifiers) have been written in capitals.
- It is a convention to write all macros in capital to identify them as symbolic constants.

```
#define X    5
```

- For above macro definition, for occurrences of X will be replaced with 5, starting from line of definition to the end of programme.
- A macro name inside a string does not get replaced.

```
e.g. Sum = X * value;
     printf("X = % d\n", X);
```

- These two lines would be changed during preprocessing as below,

```
Sum = 5 * value;
printf("X = % d\n", 5);
```

- Notice that the string "X = %d\n" is left unchanged.
- A macro definition can include more than a simple constant value.
- It can include expressions.
- Following are valid definitions.

```
#define        AREA              5*12.46
#define        SIZE              sizeof(float)*4
#define        TWO-PI            2.0*3.1415926
```

- It is good practice to use parentheses for expressions used in macro definitions.

```
#define        M                 (45 – 22)
#define        N                 (78 + 32)
```

Consider evaluation of expression,

$$\text{ratio} = \frac{M}{N}$$

it parenthesis is used result is different and if not used results would be different.

- Semicolons are not used to terminate #define statements as preprocessor replaces macro definition whenever defined macro name occurs.

Ex:

```
#define        STMT              if(a > b)
#define        AND
#define        DISPLAY           printf("a is greater \n");
```

If a statement is written as,

```
STMT AND DISPLAY
```

The preprocessor would replace the statement to if (a > b) printf("a is greater \n");

Program 1.1: Program for defining a macro using #define directive.

```
#include<stdio.h>
#define AREA length*breadth
/* macro AREA definition */
void main( )
{
    int length, breadth;
    clrscr( );
    printf("Enter the Length and Breadth\n\n");
```

```c
    scanf("%d%d",&length,&breadth);
    /* echo the data */
    printf("\nLength = %d Breadth = %d\n",length,breadth);
    printf("InArea = %d square units",AREA);
    getch( ); /* freeze the screen */
}
```

Output:

```
C:\ TC

Enter the Length and Breadth : 10 5

Length = 10
Breadth = 5
InArea = 50 square units
```

1.6 NESTED MACROS

- Macro definitions may be nested.
- Nested macro means, we can use one macro in definition of another macro.
  For example:

#define	A	5
#define	B	A + 2
#define	SQUARE (X)	((X) * (X))
#define	CUBE (X)	(SQUARE (X) * (X))
#define	TOTAL (X)	(CUBE (X) * CUBE (X))

The preprocessor expands each #define macro, until no more macros appear in the text.

For example:

(CUBE (X) * CUBE (X))

Last definition of TOTAL (X)

Last definition is first expanded into

(SQUARE (X) * (X))   *   (SQUARE (X) * (X))

CUBE (X)   CUBE (X)

Since SQUARE(X) is a macro, it is further expanded into

(((X) * (X)) * (X))   *   (((X) * (X)) * (X))

SQUARE (X)   SQUARE (X)

The final evolution of TOTAL(X) is X^6.

- Macro calls can be nested in similar way as function calls.
  For example:
  1. Given definitions of P and Q, we can define following macro to give max of 2.
     #define MAX (P,Q)   ((P) > (Q))? (P): (Q)

2. Similarly given definition of MAX (P, Q), we can use following nested call to give max of 3 values X, Y, Z.

    MAX (X, MAX (Y, Z))

Program 1.2: Program for nesting macro.

```c
#include<stdio.h>
#define SQU(x)((x)*x)
#define CUBE(x)(SQU(x)*x)
int main()
{
    int x;
    int y;
    x = SQU(3); // Argumented Macro
    y = CUBE(3); // Nested Macro
    printf("\nSquare of 3: %d",x);
    printf("\nCube of 3: %d",y);
    return(0);
}
```

Output:

Undefining a Macro:

A defined macro can be undefined using #undef statement.

Syntax: `#undef identifier`

Example: `#undef MAX (P, Q)`

This is useful when we want to restrict the definition only to particular part of program.

1.7 PARAMETERIZED MACROS

- A parameterized macro is a macro that is able to insert given parameter into its expansion.
- Each time the macroname is encountered the parameters associated with it, are replaced by actual parameters found in the program.
- It works like function with parameters so parameterized macros are also called as macro function.
- Parameters are not case sensitive, therefore we can pass any numeric variable to an argumented macro that expects a numeric argument.
- Argumented macros execute much faster as compared to similar functions.

    Syntax of parameterized macros:

    ```c
    #define identifier (f1, f2, …, fn) string
    ```

    The identifier f1, f2, …, fn are formal macro parameters that are similar to formal parameters in function definition.

- Occurrence of macro with parameter is known as macro call (similar to function call).
- Whenever a macro is called the preprocessor substitutes the string, replacing the formal parameter with actual parameters.

  Example:

  ```
  #define    CUBE(m)    (m*m*m)
  ```

  Where CUBE is macro name, m is a formal parameter and (m*m*m) is definition of macro with parameter CUBE(m)

  ```
  Volume = CUBE(side);
  ```

  If above statement appears in program, then preprocessor would expand this statement to,

  ```
  Volume = (side*side*side);
  ```

  (side*side*side) is expansion of CUBE(side) macro with actual parameter i.e. side.

Program 1.3: Program for macro with arguments.

```c
#include<stdio.h>

/* macro LARGEST definition */
#define LARGEST(a, b, c) (a>b?(a>c?a:c):(b>c?b:c))
void main( )
{
    float x=65.3, y=35.2, z=87.9, big;
    int i=41, j=91, k=11, max;
    clrscr();
    big = LARGEST(x,y,z);
    printf("Largest of %8.2f %8.2f %8.2f is %8.2f\n\n", x, y, z, big);
    max = LARGEST(i,j,k);
    printf("Largest of %8d %8d %8d is %8d\n\n", i, j, k, max);
}
```

Output:

```
C:\ TC

Largest of     65.30     35.20     87.90 is :     87.90
Largest of        41        91        11 is :        91
```

Program 1.4: Program for macros with parameters.

```c
#include <stdio.h>
#define MAX(x,y) (x>y ? x:y)
int main(void)
{
    clrscr();
    printf("\nMax between 40 and 20 is %d\n", MAX(40, 20));
    return 0;
}
```

Output:

```
C:\ TC

Max between 40 and 20 is 40
```

1.8 MACROS VERSUS FUNCTIONS

Macros	Functions
• Macros are preprocessed i.e. all macros would be processed before program complies.	• Functions are not preprocessed but compiled.
• No type checking, which can lead to errors sometimes.	• Type checking is done in function.
• Using macro increases the code length.	• Using function keeps the code length unaffected.
• Speed of execution is faster.	• Execution speed is slower.
• Before compilation, macro name is replaced by macro value.	• During function call, transfer of control takes place.
• Macros are useful when small code is repeated many times.	• Functions are useful when large code is to be written.
• Macros does not check nay compile time errors.	• Function checks compile time errors.

1.9 PRAGMA DIRECTIVES

1.9.1 #pragma Directive

- #pragma is an implementation oriented directive that allows us to specify various instructions to be given to the compiler.

  Syntax: #pragma name
  Where name is the name of pragma instruction to be given

  Example: #pragma startup
  Before the execution of main( ), the function specified in pragma is needed to run.
  #pragma exit
  Before the end of program the function specified in pragma is needed to run.

Program 1.5: Program for pragma directives.

```
#include <stdio.h>
int display();
#pragma startup display
#pragma exit display
int main()
{   printf("I am in main function");
    return 0;
}
int display()
{   printf("I am in display function");
    return 0;
}
```

Output: I am in display function
             I am in main function
             I am in display function

1.9.2 #error directive

- The #error directive is used to produce diagnostic messages during bebugging.

  Syntax: #error   error_message

  When #error directive is encountered, it displays the error message and terminates processing.

Program 1.6: Program for error directives.

```
#define BUFFER_SIZE 255
#if BUFFER_SIZE < 256
#error "BUFFER_SIZE is too small."
#endif
```

Output:

```
BUFFER_SIZE is too small.
```

1.10 CONDITIONAL COMPILATION DIRECTIVES

1.10.1 #if directive

- The #if preprocessor directive evaluates the expression or condition.
- If condition is true, it executes the code.

  Syntax:

```
#if expression
{
    stmt-1;
    stmt-2;
    --
    --
}
#end if directive
```

Program 1.7: Program for #if directive.

```
#define INDIA    1
#define COUNTRY INDIA
void main( )
{
    #if COUNTRY == INDIA
          char *currency = "Rupee";
    #endif
    clrscr();
    puts(currency) ;
}
```

Output:

1.10.2 #ifdef Directive

- The #ifdef preprocessor directive checks if macro is defined by # defined.
- If it is defined, it executes the code format.

Syntax:

```
#ifdef MACRO
{
    stmt-1;
    stmt-2;
    --

    --

}
#end ifdef directive
```

Program 1.8: Program for #ifdef directive.

```
#include<stdio.h>
#define NUM 5
void main()
{
    // Define another macro if MACRO NUM is defined
    #ifdef NUM
            #define MAX 20
    #endif
    clrscr();
    printf("\nMAX number is: %d",MAX);
}
```

Output:

1.10.3 #else directive

- The #else preprocessor directive evaluates the expression or condition of #if is false.
- It can be used with #if, #elif, #ifdef, and #ifndef directives.

Syntax:

```
#if expression
{
    // if code
}
#else
{
    // else code
}
#endif
```

Program 1.9: Program for #if, #else directives.

```c
#include <stdio.h>
#define NUMBER 1
void main()
{
    #if NUMBER == 0
    printf("value of number is %d", NUMBER);
    #else
    printf("value of number is non-zero");
    #endif

}
```

Output:

```
value of number is non-zero
```

1.10.4 #elif directive

- The #elif enables us to establish an if...else...if sequence for testing multiple conditions.

Syntax:

```c
#if expression
    // if code
#elif expression
    //if code
#else
    // else code
#end if
    --
    --
}
```

Program 1.10: Program for #elif directive.

```c
#include <stdio.h>
#define YEARS_OLD 19
int main()
{
    #if YEARS_OLD <= 10
    printf("Not eligible for voting\n");
    #elif YEARS_OLD > 10
    printf("Eligible for voting because age is %d years.\n", YEARS_OLD);
    #endif
    return 0;
}
```

Output:

```
Eligible for voting because age is 19 years.
```

1.10.5 #endif directive

- The #endif directive closes off following directives #if, #ifdef, #ifndef.
- When the #endif directive is encountered, preprocessing of opening directive #if, #ifdef, #ifndef is completed.
  Syntax: #endif

Program 1.11: Program for #endif directive.

```c
#include <stdio.h>
#define WINDOWS 1
int main ()
{   printf("Hello");
    #if WINDOWS
        pirntf(" Windows");
    #endif
        printf(" resource");
    return 0;
}
```

Output:

```
Hello windows resource
```

1.11 PREDEFINED MACROS

- A predefined macro is a macro i.e. already understood by C preprocessor without the program need to define it.
- Following are predefined macros that are provided to assist in transporting code and performing simple tasks common to many programs.

1. **_ DATE _ Macro**
- The _ DATE _ Macro evaluates to a string literal specifying the date on which compilation started.
  The _ DATE _ Macro has following syntax.
    "mm dd yyyy"
- The names of month are same as those generated by as c time library function.
  e.g.: printf("%S",_ _DATE_ _);
- The value of this macro remains constant throughout the translation unit.

2. **_ FILE _ Macro**
- The_ FILE _ Macro evaluates to a string literal specifying the file specification of the current source file.
  e.g.: printf("file %S",_ _FILE_ _);

3. **_ LINE _ Macro**
- The _LINE _ Macro evaluates to a decimal constant specifying number of line in the source file containing the macro reference.
  e.g.: printf("At line %d in file %S", _ _LINE_ _, _ _ FILE _ _);

4. _ TIME _ Macro

- The _ TIME _ Macro evaluates to a string specifying the time that the compilation started.
- The time has following format (same as the as c time function):

  hh: mm: ss

  e.g.: printf("%S", _ _ TIME _ _);
- The value of the macro remains constant throughout the translation unit.

5. _ STDC _ Macro

- The _ STDC _ Macro evaluates to a integer constant 1, which indicates a conforming implementation.
- The value of this macro remains constant throughout the translation unit.

Program 1.12: Program for predefined macros.

```c
#include <stdio.h>

int main()
{
    clrscr();
    printf("\nFile :%s\n",__FILE__);
    printf("Date :%s\n",__DATE__);
    printf("Time :%s\n",__TIME__);
    printf("Line :%d\n",__LINE__);
    return 0;
}
```

Output:

```
File :1_14.C
Date :Jan 01 2004
Time :01:14:52
Line :8
```

Summary

- A preprocessor is a program that processes or analyzes the source code file before it is given to the complier.
- File inclusion directive is the one that begins with #include which instructs compiler to include specified file.
- A macro is a small subprogram, which contains executable code.
- Preprocessor substitutes the code of macro at that position whenever macro name occurs in a program.
- #define is a preprocessor directive that defines an identifier and a value that is substituted for an identifier each time it is encountered in the source file.

- Macros and functions are having some similarities but both are having different uses.
- Apart from #include, #define there are many predefined macros which programer can use in program like #error, #progrma directives.
- There are many conditional compilation directives which makes programmer to make program execution easy to read and fast execution like #if, #endif, #else, #elif.
- There are certain predefined macros like _ DATE _, _ TIME _, _ FILE _ , _ STDC_ which will be used in program for making program easy and faster execution.

Check Your Understanding

1. A preprocessor is a program that processes or analyzed the _____ file before it is given to the _____
   - (a) machine code, linker
   - (b) source code, linker
   - (c) source code, complier
   - (d) source code, interpreter
2. _____ directive instructs compiler to include specified file.
   - (a) #include
   - (b) #if
   - (c) #define
   - (d) #elif
3. _____ is a small subprogram which contains executable code.
   - (a) function
   - (b) array
   - (c) pointer
   - (d) macro
4. To define an identifier _____ preprocessor directive is used.
   - (a) #include
   - (b) #define
   - (c) #error
   - (d) #pragma
5. #if, #endif, #else, #elif are _____ compilation directives.
   - (a) #error
   - (b) #pragma
   - (c) conditional
   - (d) #include
6. List predefined macros _____ , _____ , _____ , _____
   - (a) _DATE_,_TIME_,_FILE_, _STDC_
   - (b) #include, #error, #define, #if
   - (c) #if, #endif, #else, #elif
   - (d) None of above
7. Like other statements a preprocessor directive must end with a semicolon, state true or false.
   - (a) True
   - (b) False
8. State true or false, All preprocessor directive begin with #.
   - (a) True
   - (b) False
9. Preprocessor directive %undef can be used only on a macro that has been # define earlier.
   - (a) True
   - (b) False
10. Macro calls and function calls exactly similarly.
    - (a) True
    - (b) False

Answers

1. (c)	2. (a)	3. (d)	4. (b)	5. (c)	6. (a)	7. (b)	8. (a)	9. (a)	10. (b)

Trace The Output

1.
```c
#define WISH "Good Morning"
main()
{
    printf(WISH);
}
```
2.
```c
#define SQUARE (x)  (x*x)
main()
{
    int a = 10, b = 20, c;
    c = SQUARE (a -b);
    printf("%d",c);
}
```
3.
```c
#define M 5
main()
{
    int total, value = 10;
    total = M * value ;
    printf("M = %d", M);
    printf("Total = %d", total)
}
```
4.
```c
#define FLAG
#ifdef FLAG
    int i = 10;
#endif
main()
{
    int i = 5;
    printf("%d", i);
}
```
5.
```c
#define MAN(x, y) ((x) > (y))? (x) : (y)
main()
{
    int i=10; j=5, k=0;
    k = MAN(++i, j++);
    printf("%d %d %d \n", i, j, k);
    return 0;
}
```
6.
```c
define CUBE(x) (x * x _ x)
int main()
{
    int a, b = 3;
    a = CUBE (b++);
    printf("%d, %d \n", a, b);
    return 0;
}
```

Practice Questions

Short Answer Questions:

1. Define term macro.
2. What is preprocessor.
3. What is nested macro.
4. List preprocessor directives.
5. What is the use of #error in directives.

Long Answer Questions:

1. What is preprocessor in 'C' language? Explain with example.
2. What is macro? Explain macro substitution with example.
3. Explain nested macro in detail.
4. What are the advantages of using macro definitions in program?
5. What is file inclusion directive? When does programmer use it explain with example.
6. Differentiate between macros and functions.
7. What is conditional compilation? How it is helpful to a programmer? Explain with example.
8. Explain what is predefined macros with example.
9. Explain any four preprocessor directives.
10. Illustrate use of #itdef and #undef with examples.

Practical Assignments:

1. Define a macro PRINT that can be used to print value of any type.
2. Write a nested macro that gives minimum of three numbers.
3. Define a macro with one parameter to calculate the area of circle. Write program using this macro to calculate the area of circle using radius?
4. Define a macro PRINT and PASS integer argument and display the passed argument in the macro definition. Write a program to using this macro to display the value of passed argument.
5. Define a macro EVEN using constant value 5. Write a program using conditional compilation directive using defined macro either it's a even number or odd number.
6. Define pragma startup and end. Write a program using display function to show the execution of startup and end pragma.
7. Write a program using predefined macros to display date, time, source file name and number of lines in the program.

Previous Exam Questions

Summer 2017

1. In which stage the # include < stdio.h > gets replaced by the contents of the file stdio.h? [1]
   (a) During editing   (b) During linking
   (c) During execution   (d) During preprocessing

Ans. **(d)**

2. Find the output of the following: **[1]**
```c
# include < stdio.h >
# define int char
void main ()
}
int i = 65;
printf ("sizeof (i) = %d", sizeof(i);}
```
   (a) 2   (b) 1
   (c) 4   (d) 8

Ans. **(b)**

3. State the purpose of # error directive.   **[1]**

Ans. Refer to Section 1.9.2.

4. Differentiate between macro and function.   **[5]**

Ans. Refer to Section 1.8.

5. Write a program in C for finding the largest of 2 numbers using macro.   **[4]**

Ans. Refer Program 1.4.

6. Write any *four* predefined macros in C language   **[4]**

Ans. Refer to Section 1.11.

Winter 2017

1. What will be output of programe.   **[1]**
```c
# include < stdio.h >
# define square (x) x * x
{
    int i;
    I = 64/square (4);
    printf ("% d," i);
}
```
   (a) 4   (b) 64
   (c) 16   (d) None of the above

Ans. **(b)**

2. Give the use of # if-def with example.   **[1]**

Ans. Refer to Section 1.10.2.

3. Explain different types of preprocessor directives in C with example.   **[4]**

Ans. Refer to Section 1.4, 1.5, 1.9, 1.10.

4. Explain macro substitution in brief with example.   **[4]**

Ans. Refer to Section 1.5.

Summer 2018

1. Which of the following is macro continuation preprocessor operator.   **[1]**
   (a) #   (b) # #
   (c) /   (d) \

Ans. **(d)**

2. Which of the following is compiler control directive? [1]
   (a) # ifdef   (b) # define
   (c) # include   (d) All of the above

Ans. (a)

3. What is # pragma directive?

Ans. Refer to Section 1.9.1.

4. Compare Macro and Function. [4]

Ans. Refer to Section 1.8.

5. Explain any three predefined macros. [3]

Ans. Refer to Section 1.11.

■■■

2... Pointers

- ■ To study concept of pointer.
- ■ To learn pointer arithmetic, multiple indirection.
- ■ To learn parameter passing - call by value, call by reference.
- ■ To study dynamic memory management.
- ■ To study arrays and pointers.

2.1 INTRODUCTION

- Pointers are used in C programming as it provides many benefits to programmers.
- Pointers are more efficient in handling arrays and data tables.
- Pointers are used to return multiple values from a function through function parameters.
- Using pointer array to character strings is useful in saving storage space in memory.
- Pointers allow C to support Dynamic Memory Management.
- Pointers provide tools for manipulating data structures such as structures, linked lists, queues, stacks and trees.
- Pointers reduce length and complexity of programs.
- Pointers increase execution speed and reduce the program execution time.
- A pointer is derived data type in C.
- It is built from fundamental data types in C.
- It contains memory addresses as their value.
- It is used to access and manipulate data stored in memory.
- It is a distinct feature in C language.

2.2 CONCEPT

- Computers memory is sequential collection of storage cells, each cell is known as a byte and has a address associated with it.
- Address are numbers and numbered consecutively.

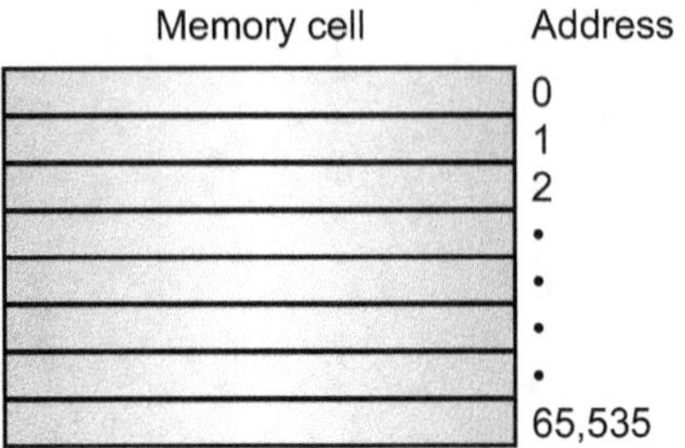

Fig. 2.1: Memory Organisation

Example: `int rollnumber=20;`

- Once variable is declared, system allocates memory cells on some memory address to hold value of variable.
- Lets consider system has allocated the address 2000 for variable rollnumber which is first byte occupied by variable rollnumber.

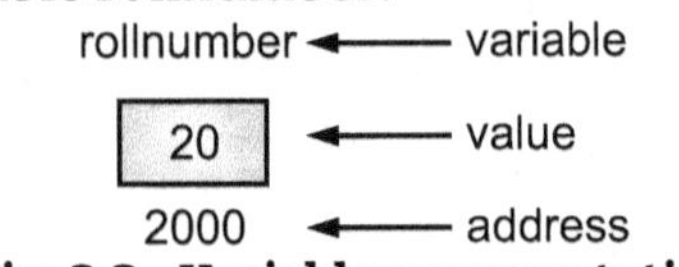

Fig. 2.2.: Variable representation

- During execution of program, system associates variable name rollnumber with address 2000.
- We can access the stored value 20 either by using variable name, rollnumber or it memory address 2000.
- As memory address are numbers they can be assigned to some variables that can stored in memory like other variable.
- Variables that holds memory addresses are called pointer variables.
- A pointer variable is a variable that contains an address, which is a location of another variable in memory.
- **Note:** As pointer is a variable its value (address of another variable) is also stored in memory on another memory address.

  Example: `int rollnumbner = 20;`

  ```
  int *ptr;
  ptr = &rollnumber;
  ```

variable	value	address
rollnumber	20	2000
ptr	2000	4050

pointer variable

Fig. 2.3

- As the value of ptr is address of variable rollnumber i.e. 2000, we can access the value of rollnumber by using the value of ptr. Hence, we may say that the variable ptr points to variable rollnumber.
- Thus ptr is called as pointer.

2.2.1 Reference and Dereference

Reference "&" Operator:
- Pointer points to address of variable where variables value is stored in memory.
- Using & ampersand operator called as reference operator "&".
- The reference operator "&" is a unary operator.
- It is used to assign the address of the variable.
- It returns the pointer address of the variable.
- So its called as referencing operator.

Example:
```
int x = 10;
int *ptr;
ptr = &x;
```
where, ptr gets the address of variable X using referencing operator "&" then pointer ptr points to address of variable X where value 10 is stored.

Deference "*" Operator:
- To fetch the value stored on the address which is pointed by pointer dereferencing operator is used.
- "*" asterisk is dereferencing operator.
- It is also called as indirection operator.
- Its a unary operator that is used for pointer variable.
- It operates on a pointer variable and returns 1 value equivalent to the value at the pointer address.

Example:
```
int x = 10; y;
int *ptr;
ptr = &x;
y = *ptr;
```
- With *ptr value will be fetched from the memory where pointer is pointing to variable address.
- In above example, pointer ptr points to address of variable x where its value 10 is stored.
- Using "*" variable y the value 10 is fetched. "*" which is a dereferencing operator.

Program 2.1: Program to understand reference operator "&" and deference operator "*"
```c
#include<stdio.h>
void main()
{
    int x = 10, y;
    int *ptr; ptr = &x;
    printf("Address of x is %u \n", &x);
    printf("Value of x is %d \n", x);
    printf("Address of ptr is %u \n", ptr);
    printf("Content of ptr is %d", *ptr);
}
```
Output:
```
Address of x is : 668
Value of x is : 10
Address of ptr is : 668
Value of ptr is : 10
```

2.2.2 Declaration

- In C programming each variable must be declared for its data type.
- As pointer variables contain addresses that belongs to separate data type they must be declared as pointer variable using same data type of variable to whom it will point.
- The pointer variable is declared using following format:

```
data_type *pointer_name;
```

- This declaration tells three things to compiler about pointer variable:
  1. The asterisk (*) called as dereferencing operator, that variable pointer_name is a pointer variable.
  2. pointer_name needs a memory location.
  3. pointer_name points to a variable of type data_type (both variable and pointer vartiable needs to be of same data type).

Example: `int * ptr;    /* integer pointer */`

Declares a variable ptr as a pointer variable that points to an integer data type variable.

(**Note:** type int refers to the data type of variable being pointed to by ptr and not the type of value of pointer).

Similarly,

```
float    *next;
```

declares next as a pointer variable to a floating point variable.

- The pointer variable is declared using symbol. Symbol can appear any where between the type name and pointer variable name.
- Following styles can be used by programmers,

```
int* next;
int * next;
int *next;
```

- However third style int *next is popular.

2.2.3 Definition

- A pointer is a variable that stores address of another variable.

Example:
```
int rollnumber = 20;
int *ptr;    /* pointer variable */
ptr = &rollnumber;
```

In above example ptr is a pointer variable as it stores the address of another variable i.e. rollnumber. And hence ptr is called a pointer to rollnumber.

2.2.4 Initialization

- The process of assigning address of a variable to a pointer variable is known as initialization.
- Once a pointer variable is declared, an assignment variable can be used to initialize the address of variable.

Example:
```
int rollnumber = 20;
int *ptr;    /* declaration */
ptr = &rollnumber;  /* intialization */
```

It is possible to combine initialization with declaration i.e.

```
int *ptr = &rollnumber
```

- It is mandatory that variable rollnumber must be declared before the initialization takes place.
- Ensure that pointer variable points to the corresponding type of data.

  Example: `float per, x;`
  ```
  int rollnumber, *ptr;
  ptr = &per;  /* wrong intialization as datatype mismatch */
  ```
  With result in wrong output as trying to assign the address of float variable to an integer pointer.
- When pointer is declared to be integer type. System assumes that any address that the pointer will hold will point to an integer variable.
- Compiler will not detect such errors so care should be taken while assigning wrong pointer.
- In one step it is possible to combine declaration of data variable, declaration of pointer variable and initialization of pointer variable.

  Example: `int rollnumber, *ptr = &rollnumber;`
  ```
  /* 3 in one in single statement */
  ```

2.2.5 Use of Pointer

- After a pointer has been assigned the address of variable, now let's see how to use a pointer, how to access the value of variable using the pointer.
- To use a pointer we have to use a *(asterisk) operator known as indirection operator or dereferencing operator.

  Example: `int rollnumbner, n;`
  ```
  int *ptr;
  rollnumber=20;
  ptr=&rollnumber;
  n=*ptr;
  ```
- In first line we have declared two variables rollnumber and n as integer type.
- On next line ptr is declared as a pointer variable pointing to integer variable.
- Next line assigns value 20 to rollnumber.
- The next line assigns address of rollnumber to pointer variable ptr.
- Next line contains the indirection operator * with pointer variable ptr.
- When * operator is palced before a pointer variable in an expression i.e. on right side of assignment operator, the pointer returns value of a variable, for which it has stored the address.
- Thus variable n contains value 20.

Program 2.2: Write a C program to show the use of pointer.

```c
#include<stdio.h>
int main()
{
    int rollnumber, x;
    int *ptr;
    rollnumber=20;
```

```
ptr=&rollnumber;
x=*ptr;
printf("value of rollnumber is %d \n", rollnumber);
printf("%d is stored at %u \n", rollnumber, &rollnumber);
printf("%d is stored at %u \n", *ptr, ptr);
printf("%d is stored at %u \n", ptr, &ptr);
printf("%d is stored at %u \n", x, &x);
*ptr = 25;
printf("\n now rollnumber = %d \n", rollnumber);
```

Output:
```
value of rollnumber is 20
20 is stored at 2010
20 is stored at 2010
2010 is stored at 2012

20 is stored at 2014

now rollnumber = 25
```

- %u gives memory address. It's a type specifier when we have to display memory address value.
- Following is memory representation of pointer assignments for above example.

Steps	Value in variables and their memory address			
	rollnumber	X	ptr	Variable
Declaration	[ ]	[ ]	[ ]	
	2010	2014	2012	address
rollnumber = 20	20	[ ]	[ ]	
	2010	2014	2012	address
ptr = &rollnumber	20	[ ]	2010	
	2010	2014	2012	address
X = *ptr	20	20	2010	
	2010	2014	2012	address
ptr = 25	25	20	2010	
	2010	2014	2012	address

2.3 TYPES OF POINTER

- Following are the types of pointers in C:
  - NULL pointer
  - Dangling pointer
  - Generic pointer
  - Wild pointer
  - Complex pointer
  - Near pointer
  - Far pointer
  - Huge pointer

2.3.1 NULL Pointer

- NULL pointer is a pointer which points nothing.
- NULL pointer points the base address of segment.
- When you don't have address to be assigned to pointer they use NULL.
- Pointer initalized with NULL value is considered as NULL pointer.
- NULL is macro constant defined in header files like stdio.h, alloc.h, mem,h, stddef.h, stdlib.h.

      defining NULL value
      #define NULL 0

  e.g. float *ptr = (float *) 0;
       char *ptr = (char *) 0;
       int *ptr = NULL;

Program 2.3: Program to illustrate NULL pointer.

```c
#include<stdio.h>
int main()
{
    int *ptr = NULL;
    printf("The value of ptr is %u", ptr);
}
```

Output:

```
The value of ptr is 0
```

2.3.2 Dangling Pointer

- Dangling pointers arise when an object is deleted or de-allocated, without modifying the value of pointer, so that pointer still points to memory location of de-allocated memory.
- i.e. pointer pointing to a non-existing memory location is called dangling pointer.

Example:

```c
#include<stdlib.h>
main()
{
    char *ptr=malloc(constant_value);

    ________

    ________

    ________
    free(ptr);          /* ptr now becomes a dangling pointer */
}
```

2.3.3 Generic Pointers

- When variable is declared as pointer to type void, it is known as generic pointer.
- Since we cannot have a variable of type void the pointer will not point to any data and therefore cannot be dereferenced. Still it's a pointer and can be used to type cast to another type of pointer.
- This type of pointer is very useful when you want to pointer to point to data of different types of different times.

Program 2.4: Program to illustrate generic pointer.

```c
#include<stdio.h>
int main()
{
    int i;
    char c;
    void *the_data;
    i=6;
    c='a';
    the_data=&i;
    printf("the_data points to integer value %d", *(int*) the_data);
    the_data=&c;
    printf("the_data points to the character %c", *(char*) the_data);
    return 0;
}
```

Output:

```
the_data points to the integer value 6
the_data now points to the character a
```

2.3.4 Generic Pointers

Wild pointer:

- A pointer in C that has not been initialized till its first use is known as wild pointer.
- A wild pointer points to some random memory location.

Example:

```c
#include<stdio.h>
main()
{
    int *ptr;
    /* ptr is a wild pointer, as it is not initialized yet */
    printf("%d", *ptr);
}
```

2.3.5 Complex Pointer

- Operator precedence describes the order in which C reads expression.

Associativity:

- Order operators of equal precedence in an expression.
- Assign priority to pointer declaration considering precedence and associative according to following table.

Operator	Precedence
(), [ ]	1
*, identifier	2
Data type	3

where, () : this operator behaves as bracket operator or function operator.

[] : this operator behaves as array subscription.

* : this operator behaves as pointer operator, not as multiplication operator.

Identifier:

- Identifier is not an operator but it is name of pointer variable always priority is assigned to name of pointer.

Datatype:

- Datatype is not an operator. Data types also include modifier.

2.3.6 Near Printer

- The pointer which can point only 64 KB data segment or segment number 8 is known as near pointer.
- This near pointer cannot access beyond the data segment like graphics video memory, text video memory etc.
- Size of near pointer is 2 byte.
- With keyword near we can make any pointer as near pointer.

Program 2.5: Program to illustrate near pointer.

```c
#include<stdio.h>
int main()
{
    int X = 25;
    int near *ptr;
    ptr = & X;
    printf("%d", sizeof(ptr));
}
```

Output:

```
2
```

2.3.7 far Pointer

- The pointer which can point or access whole residence memory of RAM i.e. which can access all 16 segment is known as far pointer.
- Size of far pointer is 4 bytes or 32 bit.

Program 2.6: Program to illustrate far pointer.

```c
#include<stdio.h>
int main()
{
    int X = 10;
    int far *ptr;
    ptr = & X;
    printf("%d", sizeof(ptr));
}
```

Output:

```
4
```

2.3.8 Huge Pointer

- The pointer which can point or access whole the residence memory of RAM i.e. which can access all 16 segment is known as a huge pointer.
- Size of huge pointer is 4 byte or 32 bit.

Program 2.7: Program to illustrate huge pointer.

```c
#include<stdio.h>
int main()
{
    char huge *far *p;
    int far *ptr;
    printf("%d %d", sizeof(p), sizeof(*p), sizeof(** p));
}
```

Output:

```
4    4    1
```

where p is huge pointer, *p is far pointer and **p is char type data variable.

2.4 POINTER ARITHMETIC

- Arithmetic operators can be used with pointers.
- Its possible to use pointer variables in expressions if they are properly declared and initialized pointers.

Example:

if P1 and P2 are properly declared and initialized pointers then following statements are valid.

```
X = *P1 ** P2 ;    /* same as (*P1) * (*P2)
Sum = sum + *P1;
```

- C programming allows us to add integers or subtract integers from pointers. As well as subtract one pointer from another pointer.
- e.g. P1 + 4, P2–2 and P1 – P2 are allowed.
- We may also use shorthand operators with pointers.

```
P1++;
–P2;
Sum + = * P2;
```

- In addition pointers can also be used with relational operators.
- Expressions such as $P_1 > P_2$, $P_1 = = P_2$ and $P_1! = P_2$ are allowed.
- We may not use pointers in division or multiplication.

Example: P_1/P_2 or $P_1 * P_2$ or $P_1/3$ are not allowed.

Similar the pointers can not be added if $P_1 + P_2$ is illegal.

Program 2.8: Program to show use of pointers in arithmetic operations.

```
#include<stdio.h>
int main()
{
    int a, b, *P1, *P2, x, y, z, x1, x2;
    a = 12;
    b = 4;
    printf("a = % d, b = % d \n", a, b);
    P1 = &a;
    P2 = &b;
    x = *P1 * P2 - 6;
    y = 4 * - *P2/*P1  + 10;
    printf("Address of a = % u \n", P1);
    printf("Address of b = % u \n", P2);
    printf("X = % d, y = % d \n", x, y);
    x1 = * P2 + 3;
    y2 = * P2 - 5;
    z = * P1 * * P2 - 6;
    printf("x1 = %d, y1 = %d", x1, y1);
    printf("z = % d \n", z);
```

Output:

```
a = 12, b = 4
Address of a = 3024
Address of b = 3026
x = 42, y = 9
x1 = 7, y1 = 7, z = 42
```

2.4.1 Multiple Indirection

- C permits the pointer to point to another pointer. This creates many layers of pointer this situation is called as multiple indirection.
- A pointer to a pointer has similar declaration like normal pointer but have more indirections i.e. more asterisk sign.

   Example:

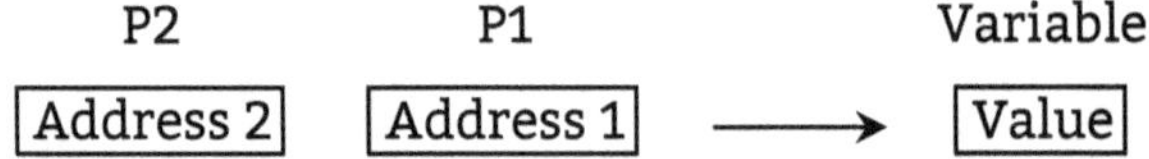

- The pointer valiable p2 contains address of pointer variable P1 which points to location where actual value of variable is stored. This is known as multiple indirections.
- A variable which is pointer to a pointer must be declared using additional indirection operator in front of the name of pointer e.g. int ** p2;
- This declaration, tells compiler that P_2 is a pointer to pointer of int type variable. P2 is not a pointer to an integer but it's a pointer to an integer pointer. To access the target value use indirection operator twice.

Program 2.9: Program 10 illustrate multiple indirection.

```c
#include<stdio.h>
int main()
{
    int m, *P₁, **P₂;
    m = 200;
    P₁ = &m;            /*  address of m */
    P₂ = &P₁;           /*  address of P₁ */
    printf("%d", **P₂);
}
```

Output:

```
200
```

2.5 PARAMETER PASSING

- Parameters can be passed to functions by using two methods:
   1. Call by value
   2. call by reference

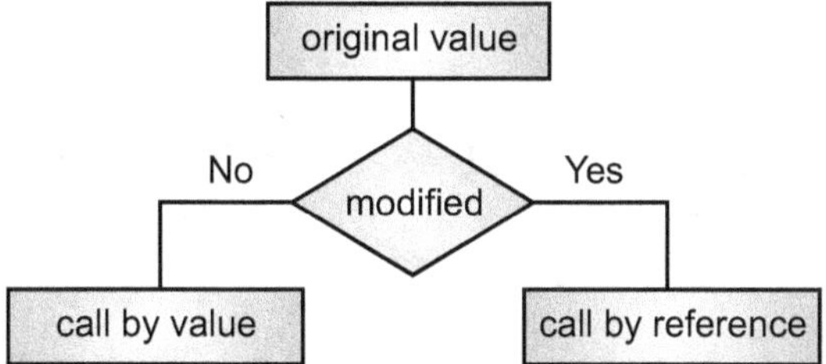

Fig. 2.4: Flowchart for parameter passing

2.5.1 Call by Value

- In call by value, value of variable is passed as parameter in function call.
- At function definition actual parameter is copied to formal parameters.
- In call by value method its not possible to modify the value of actual parameter by formal parameter.
- Different memory is allocated for actual and formal parameters.
- In call by value actual parameter is copied into formal parameter.

Program 2.10: Program for call by value.

```c
#include<stdio.h>
void change(int num)
{
    printf("Before adding value inside function num = %d \n", num);
    num=num+100;
    printf("After adding value inside function num = %d \n", num);
}
int main()
{
    int X = 100;
    printf("Before function call X = %d \n", X);
    change(X);  /* call by value */
    printf("After function call X = % d \n", X);
}
```

Output:

```
Before function call X = 100
Before adding value inside function num = 100
After adding value inside function num = 200
After function call X = 100
```

Program 2.11: Program for swapping values of two variables using call by value.

```c
#include<stdio.h>
void swap(int, int);        /*  function prototype declaration */
int main()
{
```

```c
    int a = 10;
    int b = 20;
    printf("Before swapping the values in main a = %d, b = %d \n", a, b);
    swap(a, b);    /* function call with actual values */
}
void swap (int a, int b)
{
    int temp;
    temp = a;
    a = b;
    b = temp;
    printf("After swapping values in function a=%d, b=%d \n", a, b);
}
```

Output:

```
Before swapping the values in main a = 10, b = 20
After swapping values in function a = 20, b = 10
```

2.5.2 Call by Reference

- In call by reference, address of variable is passed into function call as actual parameters.
- In call by reference the value of actual parameters can be modified by changing the formal parameters since the address of actual parameters is passed.
- In call by reference the memory allocation is similar for both formal parameters and actual parameters.
- All operations in function definition are performed on value stored at the address of actual parameters and the modified value gets stored at same address.

Program 2.12: Program for call by reference.

```c
#include<stdio.h>
void change(int *num)
{
    printf("Before adding value inside function num=%d",*num);
    *num = *num + 100;
    printf("After adding value inside function num=%d",*num);
}
int main()
{
    int x = 100;
    printf("Before function call x = %d", x);
    change(&x);    /* passing reference in function */
    printf("After function call x = %d", x);
}
```

Output:
```
Before function call x = 100
Before adding value inside function num = 100
After adding value inside function num = 200
After function call x = 200
```

Program 2.13: Program for Swapping values of two variables using call by reference.
```c
#include<stdio.h>
void swap(int *, int *);
int main()
{
    int a = 10;
    int b = 20;
    printf("Before swapping the values in main a = %d, b = %d", a, b);
    swap(&a, &b);
    printf("After swapping values in main a = %d, b=%d, \n", a, b);
}
void swap (int *a, int *b)
{
    int temp;
    temp = *a;
    *a = *b;
    *b = temp;
    printf("After swapping values in function a=%d, b=%d", *a, *b);
}
```

Output:
```
Before swapping the values in main a = 10, b = 20
After swapping values in function a = 20, b = 10
After swapping values in main a = 20, b = 10
```

2.6 ARRAYS AND POINTERS

2.6.1 Pointer to Array

- When an array is declared, compiler allocates a base address and required amount of storage to store all elements of array in contiguous memory locations.
- The base address is location of first element i.e. index 0. Ex. a[0] of the array.
- Compiler defines array name as constant pointer to first element.
  Example: int a[5] = {10, 20, 30, 40, 50};
- The memory representation of above array is as follows:

a[0]	a[1]	a[2]	a[3]	a[4]	←	Array elements
10	20	30	40	50	←	Values
2000	2002	2004	2006	2008	←	address

- As shown base address of array a is 2000. Remaining elements stored on contiguous memory location as each int required 2 bytes.
- An array name without subscript is a pointer to first element in the one, two and multidimensional array.

  i.e. a = 2000

     & a[0] = 2000
- A specified earlier compiler defined a as a constant pointer pointing to first element. So a and &a[0] is stored on location 2000.
- A pointer ptr can be used to point an array a

     ptr = a;

  is equivalent to

     ptr = &a[0];
- Its possible to access every value of a using ptr++ to move from one array element to another.
- Lets see the relation between ptr and a shown

     ptr = &a[0] = 2000

     ptr+1 = &a[1] = 2002

     ptr+2 = &a[2] = 2004

     ptr+3 = &a[3] = 2006

     ptr+4 = &a[4] = 2008
- Address of element is calculated using its index and scale factor of data type.

Example:

   address of a[3] = base address + (3 * scale factor of int)

                   = 2000 + (3 * 2) = 2006

- Pointers can be used to access array elements instead of using array elements.
- Pointer accessing method is much faster than array indexing i.e. * (ptr + 3) gives value of a[3].

Program 2.14: Program to calculate sum of all elements in an array.

```c
#include<stdio.h>
main()
{
    int *ptr, sum, i;
    int a[5] = {10, 20, 30, 40, 50};
    i = 0;
    ptr = a;  // initialising pointer with base address of a printf("Element
    value Address \n \n");
    while(i < 5)
    {
        printf("a[%d] %d %u \n", i, *ptr, ptr);
        sum=sum + *ptr;    /* Accessing array element with *p ptr */
        i++, ptr++;        /* incrementing pointer */
    }
```

```c
    printf("\n sum = %d \n", sum);
    printf("\n &a[0] = %u \n", &a[0]);
    printf("\n p = %u \n", ptr);
}
```

Output:

```
Element         Value       Address
a[0]            10          2000
a[1]                        20      2002
a[2]            30          2004
a[3]            40          2006
a[4]            50          2008
        sum  = 150
    &  a[0]  = 2000
          p  = 2010
```

- Pointers can be used to manipulate two dimensional arrays as well.
- In one dimension array a, elements a[i] can be represented using expression,
    *(a + i) or * (ptr + i)
- In two dimensional array elements can be represented using expression as,
    ((a + i)+j) or *(*(ptr + i) + j)

2.6.2 Arrays of Pointers

Array of pointers:

- We can have an array of pointer variables like an array of integer, float or char.
- As pointer variable contain an address, an array of pointers is collection of addresses.
- Pointer elements are stored in memory just like elements of other array.

    Syntax: `data_type *array name[size];`

Example:

```c
int *ptr[5];
ptr is an array of 5 integer pointers
```

Program 2.15: Program to illustrate array of pointers.

```c
#include<stdio.h>
int main()
{
    int arr[3] = {1, 2, 3};
    int i, *ptr[3];
    for(i = 0; i<3; i++)
        ptr[i] = arr + i       /* Assigning address of elements */
    for(i = 0; i < 3; i++)
    printf("address=%u \t value=%d \n", ptr[i], *ptr[i]);
}
```

Output:

```
address = 3000  Value = 1
address = 3002  Value = 2
address = 3004  Value = 3
```

Initialization of array of pointer:
- An array of pointers can be initialized during declaration as follows:

Example:
```
static int a[] = {0, 1, 2, 3, 4};
static int *p[] = {a, a+1, a+2, a+3, a+4};
int **ptr = p;
```
Above lines can be represented as:

a[0]	a[1]	a[2]	a[3]	a[4]
2000	2002	2004	2006	2008

P[0]	P[1]	P[2]	P[3]	P[4]	ptr
2000	2002	2004	2006	2008	3000
3000	3002	3004	3006	3008	4000

Example of pointers, pointers to pointer.

Array of pointers to strings.

Example:
```
char    *message[6]    =    {"Pointers",    "are",    "Intresting",    "but",    "need",
Practice"};
for(i=0; i<b; i++);
printf("%s", message[i]);
```
- Above lines can be represented as:

message[0] → | P | o | i | n | t | e | r | s | \0 |

message[1] → | a | r | e | \0 |

message[2] → | I | n | t | r | e | s | t | i | n | g | \0 |

message[3] → | b | u | t | \0 |

message[4] → | n | e | e | d | \0 |

message[5] → | P | r | a | c | t | i | c | e | \0 |

To access j^{th} character in i^{th} message *(message[i] + j)

2.7   FUNCTIONS AND POINTERS

2.7.1   Passing Pointer to Functions

- When an array is passed to a function as an argument, only the address of first element of an array is passed, but not the actual values of the array elements.

  Example: if X is an array, when a function is called like sort (X), the address of X[0] is passed to the function sort.

- Function then uses this address for manipulating the array elements.
- Similarly its possible to pass the address of variable as an argument to function.
- While passing addresses as argument to function, the receiving parameters receive address and the receiver should be a pointer.
- The process of calling a function using pointers to pass address of variables is known as call by reference.
- The function which is called by using reference can change the actual values of variable used in call.

Program 2.16: Program for passing pointer to function.

```c
#include<stdio.h>
void modify(int *, int *)    /* prototype declaration */
int main()
{
    int x1 = 20, x2 = 30;
    modify(&x1, &x2);
    printf("modified values x1 = %d, x2 = %d", x1, x2);
}
void modify(int *ptr1, int *ptr2)
{
    *ptr1 = 100;
    *ptr2 = 200;
}
```

Output:

```
modified values x1 = 100, x2 = 200
```

2.7.2 Returning Pointer from Function

- Function can return a single value by its name or return multiple values through pointer parameters
- As pointers are data types we can also force a function to return a pointer to calling function.
- The format is as follows:

```
pointer_datatype *function_name(parameter list)
```

Example: `int *f1(int);`

where f1 is a function accepting an integer and returning pointer to an integer.

Program 2.17: Program for returning pointer from function.

```c
int *larger (int *, int *);    /* function declaration */
int main()
{
    int m = 20;
    int n = 30;
```

```
    int *ptr;
    ptr = larger (&m, &n);        /* function call */
    printf("after calling function larger the value is = %d", *ptr);
}
int *larger(int *a, int *b)
{
   if(*a > *b)
        return(a);                /* address of b */
   else
        return(b);                /* address of b */
}
```

Output:

```
after calling function larger the value is = 30
```

- The function larger receives address of m and n, decides which one is larger using pointers. a & b then returns address of location. Return value is assigned to pointer variable ptr in calling function.

2.7.3 Function Pointer

- C has a powerful feature i.e. function pointer.
- Even though a function is not a variable it still has a physical memory location in memory.
- A functions address is starting address of code of function in memory. Function address assigned to a pointer is entry point to function. The pointer can be used in place of function name.
- This features allow function to be passed as argument to other functions.

   Format of declaring pointer to a function:

```
    returntype (*pointer variable) (functions_argument_list);
```

   Example: `int (*ptr) (int, int);`　　`/* ptr is pointer to a function accepting 2 integer values and returning an integer value */`

   Note: ( ) around *ptr is necessary else

```
    int * ptr (int, int);
```

   would declare ptr as a function returning a pointer to int type.

- We can make a function pointer to point to a specific function by assigning the name of function to pointer.

   Example:
```
    double (mul(int, int);
        double (*P1) ();
        P1 = mul;
```

   Declare P1 as a pointer to function and mul as function. P1 point to function mul to call function.

```
        (*P1) (x, y) is equal to mul (x, y)
```

Program 2.18: Program for pointer to function:

```c
#include<stdio.h>
int fact(int n)
{
    if(n<=1)
        return(1);
    else
        return(n*fact(n-1));
}
int main()
{
    int(*ptr) (int);    /* pointer to function with prototype of fact
                        function */
    int ans;
    int n;
    ptr = fact;         /* assigns address of fact to ptr */
    printf("Enter the number whose factorial is required");
    scanf("%d", &n);
    ans = ptr(n);       /* call to function fact using ptr */
    printf("\n the result is %d", ans);
}
```

Output:

```
Enter number whose factorial is required: 5
The result is 120
```

2.7.4 Pointers and Const

2.7.4.1 Pointer to Constant Objects

- A pointer to constant object can be declared as

  ```c
  const data_type * ptr_name.
  const int *ptr;
  ```

  Example:
  ```c
  int i = 10;
      const int *ptr;
      ptr = &i;
  ```

- ptr is a pointer to i. It means the contents pointed to by ptr cannot be changed.

  ```c
  *ptr = 20; is invalid
  ```

- However ptr itself can be changed

  ```c
  ptr++ is valid
  ```

2.7.4.2 Constant Pointers

- A constant pointer cannot be modified however data item to which it points can be modified.

  Example:
```
int i = 20;
int *const ptr;        /* declares to constant pointer ptr */
ptr = &i;
*ptr = 30;             /* valid */
ptr++;                 /* invalid */
```

- Const int *const ptr; will not allow any modification to be made to prt or the integer to which it points to.

2.8 DYNAMIC MEMORY MANAGEMENT

- Once variables and arrays are declared, explicitly memory is allocated to variables as per type and size of array.
- Such memory allocation is called static memory allocation.
- In other way programmer has to specify how much memory is required. For example, when we declare an array, we have to specify its size.
- Sometimes, we do not know how many elements are used by users, memory may be wasted or more memory is required to put more elements. This problem is solved in dynamic memory allocation method.
- We can allocate and deallocate memory at runtime is known as dynamic memory allocation.
- In C these are four library routines known as memory management functions.
- These functions help us built complex application programs that use available memory intelligently.
- The header file alloc.h contains prototypes of dynamic memory allocation functions.

Memory allocation functions:

Function	Task
`malloc()`	malloc function allocates requested size of bytes and returns a pointer to first by of allocated space.
`calloc()`	calloc function allocates space for an array of elements. It initialized all array elements to zero and then returns a pointer to memory.
`free()`	free function frees previously allocated space.
`realloc()`	realloc function modifies size of previously allocated space.

Memory allocation process:

- Following is the process to allocate memory in C program.

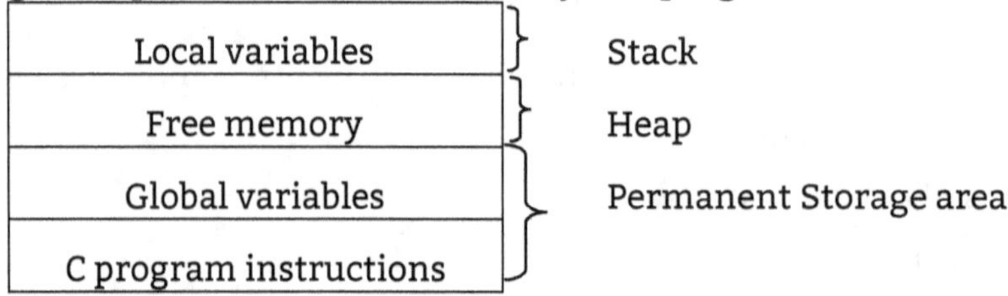

- As shown above in conceptual view of storage of program in memory. Local variables are stored in area called stack. The program instructions and global and static variables are stored in a area called as permanent storage area. The memory space between two regions is available for dynamic memory allocation during program execution known a heap.
- The size of heap keeps changing during program execution due to creation and freeing of variables that are local to functions and blocks.
- Because of this its possible to encounter memory 'overflow' during dynamic allocation process.
- In such situation above mentioned memory allocation functions return a NULL pointer.

2.8.1 Memory Allocation

- Memory can be allocated in two way:
  1. Allocating a block of memory using malloc( ).
  2. Allocating multiple blocks of memory using calloc().

1. Allocation of Block of memory using malloc

- A block of memory can be allocated using function malloc.
- It reserves a block of memory of specified size and returns pointer of void type.
- B Following is its format:

```
ptr=(cost_type*) malloc(byte_size)
```
where ptr is a pointer of cast type. The malloc returns pointer to cast type to memory area of specified byte_size.

Example: `ptr = (int *) malloc(sizeof(int));`

- After execution of this statement a memory space of 2 bytes is reserved and address of first byte to allocated memory block is assigned to pointer ptr.
- Similarly, `(ptr = (char *) malloc(20));`

During execution of this statement memory of 20 bytes will be allocated and reserves address of first byte of allocated memory is assigned to pointer (ptr of type character).

Program 2.19: Program for memory allocation using malloc().

```
#include <stdio.h>
int main()
{
    char name[100];
    char *description;
    strcpy(name, "Nirali");
    /* allocate memory dynamically */
    description = malloc( 200 * sizeof(char) );
```

```c
    if( description == NULL )
    {
        fprintf(stderr, "Error - unable to allocate required memory\n");
    }
    else
    {
        strcpy( description, "Prajakta working with Nirali Publication");
    }
    printf("\nName = %s\n", name );
    printf("Description: %s\n", description );
    return 0;
}
```

Output:
```
Name = Nirali Publication
Description: Prajakta working with Nirali Publication
```

2. **Allocating multiple blocks of memoey calloc**
- Calloc is another memory allocation function.
- It is used for allocating memory for storing derived data type such as arrays and structures.
- malloc allocates single block of storage while calloc allocates multiple block of storage each of same size.
- It sets of byte to zero.
- **Format:** `ptr = (cost_type *) calloc(n, elem_size);`
- ptr is a pointer of cast_type.
- calloc allocates contiguous space for n blocks each of size elem_size bytes.
- All bytes initialized to zero and a pointer to first byte of allocated region is returned.
- If enough space is not available a NULL pointer is returned.

  Example:
  ```c
  struct employee
  {
      char name[20];
      float age;
      int emp_id;
  };
  typedef struct employee e1;
  e1 *ptr;
  int n = 50;
  ptr = (e1 *) calloc(n, sizeof(e1));
  ```
- In above example e1 is of type struct employee having three members name, age and emp_id.
- calloc allocates memory to hold data for 50 such records.

2.8.2 Releasing Memory

Releasing allocated space using free function:

- After successful dynamic memory allocation, its need to free the allocated memory when its not required any more.
- Releasing memory after use in helpful in proper memory utilization.
- This way block of memory which is freed can be used in future.
- Memory can be released using free function.

```
free(ptr);
```

- ptr is a pointer to a memory block which has already been created by malloc or calloc.

2.8.3 Resizing Memory

Reallocating size of block: realloc

- It is possible that we can change the allocated memory size with realloc function.
- Sometimes allocated memory is less or required more memory than allocated memory.
- In both situations we can use the function realloc.

```
ptr = realloc(ptr, newsize):
```

- The above format is used if earlier allocation is done by statement

```
ptr = malloc(size);
```

- The realloc function allocates a new memory space of size newsize to pointer variable ptr and returns a pointer to first type of new memory block. Newsize may be larger or smaller than the size.

Program 2.20: Program for resizing and releasing memory.

```c
#include <stdio.h>
int main()
{
    char name[100];
    char *description;
    strcpy(name, "Pragati");
    /* allocate memory dynamically */
    description = malloc( 30 * sizeof(char) );
    if( description == NULL )
    {
        fprintf(stderr, "Error - unable to allocate required memory\n");
    }
    else
    {
        strcpy( description, "Pragati is Publication Company.");
    }
    /* suppose you want to store bigger description */
    description = realloc( description, 100 * sizeof(char) );
```

```
    if( description == NULL )
    {
        fprintf(stderr, "Error - unable to allocate required memory\n");
    }
    else
    {
        strcat( description, "Nirali is also publication company");
    }
    printf("Name = %s\n", name );
    printf("Description: %s\n", description );
    /* release memory using free() function */
    free(description);
    return 0;
}
```

Output:

```
Name = Pragati
Description: Pragati is Publication Company. Nirali is also publication
company
```

2.9   DANGLING POINTERS / MEMORY LEAK

- If a pointer still references the original memory after it has been freed, it is called a dangling pointer.

- The pointer does not point to a valid object. This is sometimes referred to a premature free.

- A dangling pointer occurs when you are pointing to an object or other area of memory that is not valid anymore. In C, this may happen for several reasons, such as accessing a pointer that was freed.

- A memory leak is a point of a program where some memory becomes inaccessible, even though it was not released by the system. Memory leaks are possible in C, only changing the mechanism by which memory is released.

- A dangling pointer is a pointer to storage that is being used in for another purpose. Typically, the storage has been deallocated. Operation dispose(p) leaves 'p' dangling.

- Storage that is allocated but in inaccessible is called garbage. Programs that create garbage are said to have memory leaks. Assignment to pointers can lead to memory leak.

- For example: Suppose a and b are pointers to cells. The pointer assignment,

    a: = b

Leaves a and b pointing to same cell.

- The cell that b was pointing to, as shown in Fig. 2.9.

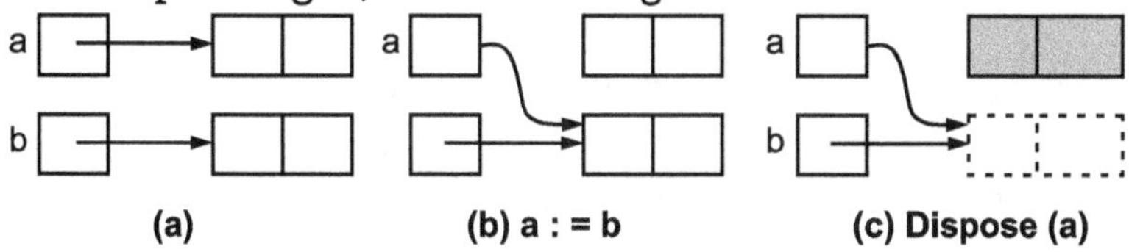

Fig. 2.5: Pointer Assignment can Result in the Memory Leak and Dispose can Result in Dangling Pointers

- The cell that 'a' pointed to is still in memory, but it is inaccessible, so we have a memory leak. Now, **dispose(a)**deallocates the cell that 'a' points to. It leaves 'a' and 'b' both dangling, since they both point to same cell.

Summary

- Pointer variable is nothing but a variable that contains an address of another variable in memory.
- Types of pointer specifies details of how pointer can be used in different ways to make program execution easy and fast.
- Pointer arithmetic gives details of how pointer variables can be used in expression.
- Multiple indirection pointer variable contains address of another pointer variable which points to location that contains desired value.
- Call by value, call by reference gives details about parameter passing ways.
- Functions and pointers given details of how pointer can be passed to function, how we can return pointer from function etc.
- Arrays and pointers gives details of pointer to array and how array of pointer can be used.
- Dynamic memory allocation functions can be used to allocate single block, multiple block, reallocating and freeing memory.

Check Your Understanding

1. A pointer variable contains as its value ______ of another variable.
   - (a) value
   - (b) address
   - (c) operator
   - (d) none of above
2. The ______ operator returns the value of variable to which its operand points.
   - (a) &
   - (b) *
   - (c) ·
   - (d) none of above
3. The only integer that can be assigned to a pointer variable is ______.
   - (a) 1
   - (b) 2
   - (c) 0
   - (d) none of above
4. The pointer that is declared as ______ cannot be dereferences.
   - (a) int
   - (b) void
   - (c) both (a) and (b)
   - (d) none of above

5. Pointer constants are addresses of memory locations.
    (a) True   (b) False
6. Pointer variables are declared using address operator.
    (a) True   (b) False
7. A pointer can never be subtracted from another pointer.
    (a) True   (b) False
    (a) True   (b) False
8. Pointers cannot be used as formal parameters in headers to function definitions.
    (a) True   (b) False
9. When an array is passed as an argument to a function, a pointer is passed.
    (a) True   (b) False

Answers

1. (b)	2. (b)	3. (c)	4. b)	5. (b)	6. (b)	7. (b)	8. (b)	9. (a)

Trace Output

1.
```c
main()
{
    char * ptr = "machine";
    printf("%s", x++);
    printf("%c", ++*   ++x);
    printf("%s", ++x);
}
```

2.
```c
main()
{
    int i = 20, *ptr = &i;
    char * ptrc = "abcd";
    printf("%d \%d", size of (ptr), size of (ptr c));
}
```

3.
```c
main()
{
    char *ch;
    int *i;
    float *f;
    double *d;
    printf("%u  ch+1=%u", ch, ch+1);
    printf("\n i=y i+1=%u", i, i+1);
    printf("\n f = %u f + 1 = %u", f, f+1);
    printf("\n d=%u d+1 = %u", d, d+1);
}
```

Practice Questions

Short Answer Questions:

1. What is pointer? How is pointer initialized?
2. What is pointer? List types of pointer?
3. What is referencing operator?
4. What is dereferencing operator?
5. What is call by value?

Long Answer Questions:

1. Explain types of pointer in detail with example.
2. What is multiple indirection? Explain with example.
3. What is call by reference.
4. How to use pointer to array explain?
5. How to pass pointer to function.
6. What is array of pointer? Explain.
7. Explain how to return a pointer from function.
8. What is function pointer concept?
9. Explain concept pointers and constant.
10. What is dynamic memory allocation explain with example.
11. Explain dynamic memory allocation functions with its syntax and example.

Previous Exam Questions

| Summer 2017 |

1. What will be output of program.   [1]

```c
# include < stdio.h >
int main ( )
{
int i = 3, * j, k ;
j = & i;
printf ("% d\n", i* *j * + *j);
return 0;
```

   (a) 30   (b) 27
   (c) 9   (d) 3

Ans. (b)

2. The function used to release previously allocated space from memory is: **[1]**

    (a) malloc   (b) Free

    (c) release   (d) none

Ans. **(b)**

3. How can a pointer to pointer be declared?   **[1]**

Ans. Refer to Section 2.4.1.

4. Write a program using pointer to array concept to add two 1D arrays store addition in third array.   **[5]**

Ans. Refer Chapter 2.6.1.

5. Write a note on Dynamic memory allocation.   **[4]**

Ans. Refer to Section 2.8.

6. Explain the purpose of each of the following declaration: **[3]**

    (i) int(*x) (int *a);

    (ii) int(*a) (int, int);

    (iii) int(*p) (char);

Ans. Refer Section 2.2.2.

7. Find the output of the following.   **[3]**

```c
main ( )
{
int a = 10, b = 15;
change (a, & b)
printf ("%d %d", a, b) ;
}
change (int x, int *y)
{
x = 20;
*y = 30;
}
```

Ans. If we consider syntax error then after change() method require semicolon without considering any syntax error output is 10 30 .

Winter 2017

1. A pointer is: **[1]**

    (a) A keyword used to create variables

    (b) A variable that stores address of an instruction

    (c) a variable that stores address of other variable

    (d) All of the above

Ans. **(c)**

3. What is the use of void pointer? **[1]**

Ans. Void pointers are used to implement generic function in c.

4. Define pointer. Explain how to declare, initialize and use a pointer (de-referencing pointer). **[5]**

Ans. Refer to Section 2.2.

5. Write a short note on pointer to function. **[3]**

Ans. Refer to Section 2.7.1.

6. Explain the function used to allocate and deallocate memory dynamically. **[5]**

Ans. Refer to Section 2.8.

7. Write a C program to find sum of n elements entered by user. To perform this program, allocate memory dynamically using malloc() function. **[4]**

Ans. Refer Program 2.19.

8. Explain pointer-to-pointer concept with suitable example. **[3]**

Ans. Refer to Section 2.4.1.

Summer 2018

1. Trace the output **[1]**
   char str[20] = "Bye";
   printf ("% C", * srt);
   (a) Bye   (b) B
   (c) y   (d) Error

Ans. **(b)**

2. If variable is a pointer to a structure, then which of the following operator is used to access data members of the structure. **[1]**
   (a) &   (b) •
   (c) *   (d) →

Ans. **(d)**

3. Define pointer to pointer. **[1]**

Ans. Refer to Section 2.4.1.

4. What do you mean by 'Array of pointers' and 'pointer to array'? Explain with an example. **[5]**

Ans. Refer to Section 2.6.2.

5. Trace the output and Justify. **[3]**

```c
int main( )
{
    static char s [ ] = "Tendulkar" ;
    char * P ;
    while (* P)
        printf (" % C * p++") ;
}
```

Ans. It generates an error Segmentation fault because pointer does not have any value.

6. Explain 'Function returning pointer' concept. [4]

Ans. Refer to Section 2.7.2.

7. Define dynamic memory Allocation. What are the advantages of dynamic memory allocation over static allocation? [4]

Ans. Refer to Section 2.8.

8. Explain the purpose of each of the following. [3]
declarations

(i)　int *P [5]

(ii)　int f1 (int *P [ ])

(iii) int * f2 (int *P [])

Ans. Refer to Sections 2.2.2

■■■

3...
Strings

- ▣ To understand what is a string and how to declare, define and initialize string.
- ▣ To learn how to read and write string from console.
- ▣ To know importance of terminating character.
- ▣ To understand how strings and pointers work.
- ▣ To understand what is array of strings and what is array of character pointer.
- ▣ To learn use of string in user defined function.
- ▣ To know more about the different predefined functions in string.h.

3.1 INTRODUCTION

- A string is a collection of characters under a single name.
- Group of characters defined between double quotation marks is a string constant e.g. "NIRALI PRAKASHAN IS BEST".
- Strings are used in building readable programs.
- Many operations are performed on character strings like reading, writing, correcting, copying, comparing and extracting portion of string.

3.2 CONCEPT

- A string is a collection of characters in sequence.
- This collection is treated as a single data item.

3.2.1 Declaration and Definition of String

- Using char data type we can declare a character.
- In C programming there is no special data type to declare a string.
- To declare a string char data type has to be used with an array of characters.
- The syntax of declaration of a string variable is,

```
char string_name[size];
```

- The size determines number of characters in string_name.
- string_name is a variable name needs to be a valid C variable name.

Example: `char name[20];`
  `char name[50];`

- The above declaration is stored in memory as:

0	1	2	3	4	5	6	7	8	9						19	for name

0	1	2	3	4	5	6	7	8	9						49	for address

- If we store value in string name as "NIRALI PRAKASHAN".
- Compiler assigns a string to a character array name. It automatically supplies a null character '\0' at the end of string.
- Therefore the size should be equal to max number of character in string plus one for null character '\0'.
- The above declaration stores the name in memory is as follows:

0	1	2	3	4	5	6	7	8	9	10	11	12	13	14	15	16	17	18	19
N	I	R	A	L	I		P	R	A	K	A	S	H	A	N	\0	\0	\0	\0

3.2.2 Initialization String Variables

- Character arrays can be initialized like numeric arrays.
- We can initialize array after declaration or initialized at the time of declaration.
  Example: `address[12] = "MUMBAI PUNE";`
    `char city[20] = {'B', 'A', 'N', 'G', 'L', 'O', 'R', 'E', '\0'};`
- In first example, Address is declared with size 12 elements long as initialized strings contains 11 characters and one element space is provided for null terminator.
- We have used null terminator in first example as it implicitly supply null terminator '\0'. Just need to keep one space for null terminator.
- In second example, we have listed its elements using curly bracket. Each character has to be enclosed in single quotation.
- All elements to be separated by using(,) operator.
- The last character is null terminator, which must be supplied explicitly as shown above.
- C permits to initialize a character array without giving size i.e. number of elements.
- In this case size of array will be determined automatically based on elements initialized.
  Example: `char wish[ ] = {'B', 'E', 'S', 'T', ' ', 'W', 'I', 'S', 'H', 'E', 'S', '\0'};`
- Its possible to declare string array size larger.
  Example: `char str[10] = "HELLO";`
- It gets array of size 10, places to value "HELLO" in it adds null character after HELLO and initializes all other elements to NULL.

0	1	2	3	4	5	6	7	8	9
H	E	L	L	O	\0	\0	\0	\0	\0

- Following declaration is wrong:
    ```
    char str[3] = "Good";
    ```
    this will generate compile time error.
    ```
    char str3[5];
    str3 = "GOOD";
    ```
    is not allowed as we cannot separate the initialization from declaration.

3.2.3 Format Specifier

- We use %s format specifier to read in string of characters.
- We use %s with input function scanf.
    Example: `char name[10];`
    `scanf("%s", name);`
- In case of character arrays the ampersand (&) is not required before variable name like other type of variables.
- Scanf function terminates its input on first white space it finds.
- White space includes blanks, tabs, carriage returns, form feeds and new lines.
    Example: Hello everyone
- It reads only Hello into name array since the blank space after the word Hello will terminates heading of string with a null character.

Program 3.1: Program for format specifiers.
```
#include<stdio.h>
main()
{
    char ch;
    char name[10];
    printf("Enter a character \n");
    scanf("%c", &ch);
    printf("Enter name \n");
    scanf("%s", &name);
    printf("%c %s", ch, name);
    getch();
}
```
Output:
```
Enter a character
C
Enter name
Deepali
C Deepali
```

3.2.4 String Literals/Constants & Variables

- String literal is a sequence of zero or more characters.
- String literals are enclosed in double quotes " ".

- A string contains characters that are similar to character literals i.e. plain characters, escape sequence and universal characters.
- Its possible to break a long line into multiple lines using string literals and separating them using white spaces.

  Example:

  ```
  "hello, friends"
  "hello, \friends"
  "hello," "f"  "friends"
  ```
- String literals is also known as string constant or constant string.
- String literals are stored in C as an array of characters and terminated by null byte, i.e. '0'.
- Character strings are often used in programs to build meaningful programs.

String variables:

- String variables are stored as array of characters terminated by a null byte '\0'.
- String variables can be initialized either with individual character or more commonly with string literals.

  ```
  char str[ ] = {'h', 'e', 'L', 'L', 'O', '\0'};
  char str1[] = "hello";
  char str1[20] = "hello";
  ```

3.3 READING AND WRITING FROM AND TO CONSOLE

3.3.1 Reading String from Console

1. **Using scanf() function:**
- Like other data type variables, string variables read from terminal using scanf() function.
- %S format specifier is used to read in a string of characters.

  Example: `char address[10];`

  ```
              scanf("%s", address);
  ```
- For character arrays the ampersand (&) is not required before the variable name.
- scanf function automatically terminates the string that is read with a null character and therefore the character array should be large enough to hold the input string plus the null character.

Program 3.2: Program to read a series of words i.e. strings from terminal using scanf function.

```c
#include<stdio.h>
main()
{
    char str1[30], str2[30], str3[30], str4[30];
    printf("Enter string values \n");
    scanf("%s %s",str1, str2);
```

```
    scanf("%s %s",str3, str4);
    printf("\n string1=%s \n string2 = %s \n", str1, str2);
    printf("\n string3=%s \n string4 = %s \n", str3, str4);
}
```

Output:

```
Enter string values
Prajkta Khatavkar Pranjal Waghmare
string 1 = Prajakta
string 2 = Khatavkar
string 3 = Pranjal
string 4 = Waghmare
```

Reading string specifying field width

- We can specify the field width using form %ws in scanf statement for reading a specified number of characters from input string.

  Example: `scanf("%ws", name);`
- While using width field remember the things.
- The width is greater than or equal to the string read in. In this case entire string will be stored in string variable.
- The width is less than the string width. In this case excess characters than width will be truncated and left unread.

  Example: `char name[10];`

  `          scanf("%5s", name);`
- Let consider input string is NIT, will be stored as:

0	1	2	3	4	5	6	7	8	9
N	I	T	\0	\0	\0	\0	\0	\0	\0

  i.e. width field is greater than specified width.
- Let consider input string is SATYAM, will be stored as

0	1	2	3	4	5	6	7	8
S	A	T	Y	A	M	\0	\0	\0	\0

  i.e. field width is less than specified with so sixth character is truncated.

2. **Using getchar() function:**

- getchar function is used to read a single character from terminal.
- Using getchar we can read character from terminal and place it into character array.
- This needs to be done repeatedly to read in, line of text and stored in an array.
- The reading of character is terminated when newline character '\n' is entered so null character is then inserted at the end of string.
- The syntax of getchar is,

  ```
  char ch;
  ch = getchar();
  ```
- It has no parameters.

3. Using gets() function:

- gets function is convenient method of reading a string containing white spaces from terminal.
- gets function is available in <stdio.h> header file.

  Syntax: `gets(string_variable);`

  where string_variable is parameter for which gets function reads string from keyboard until newline character is encountered then appends null character to string.
- gets function never skip white space i.e. white space is allowed while reading string.
- This is not possible with scanf where white space terminates string.

  Example: `char line[80];`
  `gets(line);`
  `printf("%s", line);`

  Reads a line of text from keyboard and displays it on screen.

3.3.2 Writing string to Console

1. Using printf() function:

- printf function is used to display string to screen.
- %s format specification is used to display i.e. an array of characters that is terminated by null character.

  Example: `printf("%s", name);`
- Above statement is used to display contents of array name.
- Along with %s we can specify width and we can specify precision for the array to display.

  Example: % 10.4

  which says that display first four characters in the field width of 10 columns.
- We can add '–' minus sign in the specification.

  Example: % - 10.4 s

  The string will be displayed / printed in left justification.

Program 3.3: Program to store string "NIRALI PRAKASHAN" in array name.

```c
#include<stdio.h>
void main()
{
    char name[20] = "NIRALI PRAKASHAN";
    printf("\n \n");
    printf("%16s \n", name);
    printf("%5s \n", name);
    printf("%16.5s \n", name);
    printf("%16.6s\N", name);
    printf("%16.0s\N", name);
    printf("%.3s\N", name);
    printf("%s \n", name);
}
```

Output:

```
NIRALI PRAKASHAN
NIRALI PRAKASHAN
        NIRAL
        NIRALI
NIR
```

- When field width is less than the length of string, the entire string is displayed.
- The integer value on the right side of decimal point specifies the number of characters to be printed.
- When number of characters to be printed is specified S zero nothing is displayed.
- The minus sign in specification caused the string to be printed left-justified.
- The specification %ns prints first n characters of the string.

2. **Using putchar() functions**

- Like getchar function putchar function is used to display values of character variable.
- It syntax is:

```c
char ch = '4';
putchar(ch);
```

- putchar requires one parameter.
- Using putchar repeatedly its possible to display string of characters stored in array.

   Example:
```c
char name[20] = "NIRALI PRKASHAN";
for (i = 0; i < 10; i++);
putchar(name[i]);
```

Program 3.4: Program for getchar and putchar functions.

```c
#include<stdio.h>
int main()
{
    int c;
    clrscr();
    printf( "Enter a value:");
    c = getchar();
    printf( "\nYou entered: ");
    putchar( c );
    return 0;
}
```

Output:

3. Using puts() function:

- Using puts we can display string value.
- puts declared in header file<stdio.h>.
- This function syntax is:

      puts(array_name);

  where, array_name variable containing string value.
- This displays the value of string variable array_name.

  Example: puts(name)

Program 3.5: Program for gets and puts functions.

```c
#include<stdio.h>
int main()
{
    char str[100];
    clrscr();
    printf("Enter a string:");
    gets(str);
    printf("\nYou entered: ");
    puts( str );
    return 0;
}
```

Output:

Program 3.6: Program for scanf and printf functions.

```c
#include<stdio.h>
int main()
{
    char str[100];
    int i;
    clrscr();
    printf("Enter a value:");
    scanf("%s %d", str, &i);
    printf("\nYou entered: %s %d ", str, i);
    return 0;
}
```

Output:

3.4 IMPORTANCE OF TERMINATING NULL CHARACTER

- In C programming compiler assigns a character string to character array, it automatically supplies null character '\0' at the end of string. This terminating character plays important role as follows.
- Like other data types string is not a data type in C. It is considered as a data structure stored in array.
- String is variable-length structure and is stored in fixed length array.
- The array size is not always the size of string array size.
- Sometimes is smaller or sometime array size is much larger than string stored in it. Therefore last element of array need not represent end of string. It is necessary to determine the end of string data.
- NULL character serves as end-of-string marker i.e. terminating character.
  Example: char string[] = {'H', 'E', 'L', 'L', 'O', '\0'};
- The above statement defines array string of 5 elements.

```
char str[10] = "GOOD";
```

0	1	2	3	4	5	6	7	8	
G	O	O	D	\0	\0	\0	\0	\0	\0

- In above case 10 characters size is created where value is placed in it, terminates with null character and initialized to NULL other element.

3.5 STRINGS AND POINTERS

- Strings are character arrays, so they can be declared and initialized as,
  ```
  char name[5] = "SITA";
  ```
- Compiler automatically inserts null character '\0' at the end of string.
- C supports alternate method to create string using pointer variables of the type char.
  Example: char * name = "SITA";
- This statement creates a string for literal and stores its address in Pointer variable name.
- Pointer name points to first character of string "SITA" as

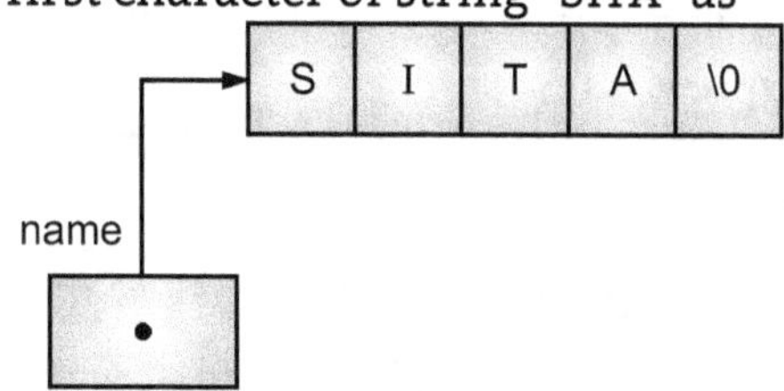

- It is allowed to do runtime assignment for giving values to string pointer name,
  Example: char *name;
  ```
  name="SITA";
  ```
- Above statement name="SITA" is not string copy statement as name is a pointer not a string.

- We can display contents of name using output functions like printf/puts.

  Example: `printf("%s", name);`

          `puts(name);`

- Along with "name" pointer indirection/deference operator * is not allowed to use even it is pointer to string, it is also name of string.

- It is possible to use a pointer to access individual characters in a string.

Program 3.7: Program using pointers to calculate length of string.

```c
#include<stdio.h>
void main()
{
    char *name;
    int length;
    name="PUNE";
    char *ptr = name;
    printf("%s \n", name);
    while(*ptr != '\0')
    {
        printf("%C is stored at address %u \n", *ptr, ptr);
        ptr++;
    }
}
```

Output:

```
PUNE
P is stored at address 50
U is stored at address 51
N is stored at address 52
E is stored at address 53
```

3.6 ARRAY OF STRINGS

- An array of strings is a two-dimensional array.

- Array of string is required in application where list of names is required like student list, employee list. It is even called as "table of string".

- A list of names can be treated as table of strings.

- Two dimensional character array can be used to store to entire list.

  Example: an array of string for students list,

  `char student [3] [5];`

- This is used to store list of 3 names, each of length not more than 5 characters as shown below:

	0	1	2	3	4
student[0]	Y	A	S	H	\0
student[1]	H	A	N	S	\0
student[2]	R	A	M	\0	

- As declared above array of strings i.e. two dimensional array, above declaration will be stored in table form.
- To access name of ith student in the list we have to write student [i – 1].
- So student[0] denote "YASH", student[1] denotes "HANS" and so on.
- Array of strings can be treated as column of strings.

Program 3.8: Programs to sort list of names in alphabetical order using array of strings.

```c
#define ITEMS 5
#define MAX CH 20
main()
{
    char string[ITEMS] [MAXCH], temp[MAX CH];
    int m=0, n=0;
    printf("Enter names of %d items \n", ITEMS);
    while(m < ITEMS)
    scanf("%s", string[m++]);
    for(m=1; m<ITEMS; m++)
    {
        for(n=1; n<=ITEMS-m; n++)
        {
            if(strcmp(string[n - 1],string[n]) > 0)
            {
                strcpy(temp, string[n - 1]);
                strcpy(string[n - 1], string[n]);
                strcpy(string[n], temp);
            }
        }
    }
    printf("\n Alphabetical list is \n");
    for(m=0; m<ITEMS; m++)
    printf("\n %s", string[m]);
}
```

Output:

```
Enter names of 5 items
PUNE BOMBAY NANDED AURANGABAD AKOLA
Alphabetical list is
AKOLA
AURANGABAD
BOMBAY
NANDED
PUNE
```

3.6.1 Array of Character Pointers

- An array of pointers is a two dimensional array. This concept is important use of pointer in handling table of strings.
- Consider an array of strings,

```
char name[3][25];
```

- The above statement declares name table containing three names each with maximum 25 characters. This requires 75 bites storage space in memory.
- Most of the times allocated memory bites are not completely utilized. So instead of making each row with a fixed no. of characters, we can make it a pointer to string of varying length.

  Example:

```
char *name[3] = {"Yash Bhoskar",
                 "Shrayas Bhoskar",
                 "Nikhil Bhoskar"};
```

- Above declaration declares name to be an array of 3 pionters to characters where each pointer is pointing to a particular name as follows:

```
name[0]  →  Yash Bhoskar
name[1]  →  Shrayas Bhoskar
name[2]  →  Nikhil Bhoskar
```

- This declaration allocates only 41 bites which is sufficient to hold all characters as shown.

Y	a	s	h		B	h	o	s	k	a	r	\0			
S	h	r	a	y	a	s		B	h	o	s	k	a	r	\0
N	i	k	h	i	l		B	h	o	s	k	a	r	\0	

- To print all three names following statements are used:

```
for(i = 0; i <=2; i++)
    printf("%s \n", name[i]);
```

3.7 USER DEFINED FUNCTIONS

- We will learn to create our own string based function to get the length of the string, to reverse the string, to copy string, compare two strings with ad without checking case, to extract a portion of string (extracting substring), splitting string and many more.

Pragram 3.9: Count the total number of characters available in a string and without using strlen() function.

```c
#include <stdio.h>
int stringLength(char*);
int main()
{
    char str[100]={0};
    int length;
    printf("Enter any string: ");
    scanf("%s",str);
    /*call the function*/
    length=stringLength(str);
    printf("String length is: %d\n",length);
    return 0;
}
/*function definition...*/
int stringLength(char* txt)
{
    int i=0,count=0;
    while(txt[i++]!='\0')
    {
        count+=1;
    }
    return count;
}
```

Output:

```
Enter any string: Prajakta
String length is: 8
```

Program 3.10: Read a string and copy the string into another without using stringCopy() function.

```c
#include <stdio.h>
void stringCpy(char* s1,char* s2);
int main()
{
    char str1[100],str2[100];

    printf("Enter string 1: ");
```

```c
    scanf("%[^\n]s",str1);//read string with spaces

    stringCpy(str2,str1);

    printf("String 1: %s \nString 2: %s\n",str1,str2);
    return 0;
}

/******** function definition *******/
void stringCpy(char* s1,char* s2)
{
    int i=0;
    while(s2[i]!='\0')
    {
        s1[i]=s2[i];
        i++;
    }
    s1[i]='\0'; /*string terminates by NULL*/
}
```
Output:
```
Enter string 1: Prajakta
String 1: Prajakta
String 2: Prajakta
```

Program 3.11: Read a string from the user, and convert the string into lowercase and uppercase without using the library function.

```c
#include <stdio.h>
void stringLwr(char *s);
void stringUpr(char *s);
int main()
{
    char str[100];
    printf("Enter any string: ");
    scanf("%[^\n]s",str);//read string with spaces
    stringLwr(str);
    printf("String after stringLwr: %s\n",str);
    stringUpr(str);
    printf("String after stringUpr: %s\n",str);
    return 0;
}

/******** function definition *******/
void stringLwr(char *s)
{
    int i=0;
```

```c
        while(s[i]!='\0')
        {
            if(s[i]>='A' && s[i]<='Z'){
                s[i]=s[i]+32;
            }
            ++i;
        }
    }
    void stringUpr(char *s)
    {
        int i=0;
        while(s[i]!='\0')
        {
            if(s[i]>='a' && s[i]<='z'){
                s[i]=s[i]-32;
            }
            ++i;
        }
    }
```

Output:
```
Enter any string: Prajakta
String after stringLwr: prajakta
String after stringUpr: PRAJAKTA
```

Program 3.12: Read a two string from the user and concatenate them without using the library function.

```c
    #include <stdio.h>
    #include <string.h>
    #define MAX_SIZE 100
    void stringCat (char *s1,char *s2);
    int main()
    {
        char str1[MAX_SIZE],str2[MAX_SIZE];
        printf("Enter  string 1: ");
        scanf("%[^\n]s",str1);//read string with spaces
        getchar();//read enter after entering first string
        printf("Enter  string 2: ");
        scanf("%[^\n]s",str2);//read string with spaces
        stringCat(str1,str2);
        printf("\nAfter concatenate strings are:\n");
        printf("String 1: %s \nString 2: %s",str1,str2);
        printf("\n");
        return 0;
    }
    /******** function definition *******/
```

```c
void stringCat (char *s1,char *s2)
{
    int len,i;
    len=strlen(s1)+strlen(s2);
    if(len>MAX_SIZE)
    {
        printf("\nCan not Concatenate !!!");
        return;
    }
    len=strlen(s1);
    for(i=0;i< strlen(s2); i++)
    {
        s1[len+i]=s2[i];
    }
    s1[len+i]='\0'; /* terminates by NULL*/
}
```

Output:

```
Enter string 1: prajakta
Enter string 2: khatavkar
After concatenate strings are:
String 1: prajaktakhatavkar
```

3.8 PREDEFINED FUNCTIONS IN String.h

1. **strlen() function**
- This function is used to count number of characters in a string after counting function returns the count.

   Syntax: `int_variable = strlen(string);`

   where integer variable is the one which receives the value of length of string returned by strlen function.
- The string is the argument for which function counts no. of characters in the string which may be a string constant.
- A counting ends at 1st null character.

   Example: `int x;`
   ` char name[ ] = "Deepali";`
   ` x = strlen(name);`
- X will be 7 as the name string contains total 7 characters, so strlen returns value 7 assigned to integer variable X.

2. **strcpy() function:**
- This function is similar to string assignment operator.
- This function assigns contents of string2 to string1 where string2 may be a character array variable or a string constant.

Syntax: `strcpy(string1, string2);`
Example: `strcpy(pune city, "PUNE");`
will assign the string "PUNE" to string variable city.
- Similarly the statement,

        `strcpy(city1, city2)`

will assign the contents of the string variable city2 to the string variable city1. The size of the array city1 should be large enough to receive the contents of city2.

3. **strcat() function:**
- This function is used to concatenate or join strings together.
  Syntax: `strcat(string1, string2)`
  where string1 and string2 are character arrays.
- After successful execution of strcat string2 is appended to string1.
- While combining 1st null character is removed at the end of string one and placing string2 thereafter. In this case string2 remains unchanged.
  Example: `strcat(part1, part2);`
  while using strcat make sure that size of string1 should be declared large enough to accommodate string2.
- strcat function also appends a string constant to a string variable.

      `strcat(part1, "GOOD");`

  C permits nesting of strcat function.
  Example: `strcat(strcat(string1, string2), string3);`
- In concatenates all three strings together and the result is stored in string1.

4. **strcmp() function:**
- This function compares 2 strings and returns value 0 if they are equal.
  Syntax: `strcmp(string1, string2)`
  string1 and string2 may be string variables or string constant.
  Example: `strcmp(name1, name2);`

          `strcmp(name1, "John");`
          `strcmp("Rom", "Ram");`

Program 3.13: Program to show use of all above pre-defined string functions:

```c
#include<string.h>
main()
{
    char s1[20],s2[20],s3[20];
    int x, l1, l2, l3;
    printf("\n\nEnter two string constants \n");
    scanf("%s %s", s1, s2);
    /* comparing s1 and s2 */
    X = strcmp(s1, s2);
```

```c
        if(x! = 0)
        {
            printf("\n \n strings are not equal \n");
            strcat(s1,s2);    /* joining s1 and s1 */

        }
        else
        printf("|n \n strings are equal \n");
        /*  copying s1 and s3
            strcpy(s3, s1);
        /* finding length of string  */
            l1 = strlen(s1);
            l2 = strlen(s2);
        /* Output */
            printf("\n s1 = % s \t length = % d characters \n", s1, l1);
            printf("s2 = % s \t length = % d characters \n", s2, l2);
    }
```

Output:

```
    Enter two strings constants
    New York
    Strings are not equal
    s1 = New York    length = 7 characters
    s2 = York        length = 4 characters
```

5. **strnset():**
* It sets the portion of characters in a string to given character.

    Syntax: `char * strnset(char * string, char C, int n);`

    where string is original string, C is given character, n is no. of characters to be replaced.

Program 3.14: Program to show use of strnset()

```c
    #include<stdio.h>
    #include<string.h>
    main()
    {
        char str[20]; = "Test string";
        printf("original string is % s", str);
        printf("Test string after string n set %s", strnset(str, '#', 4));

    }
```

Output:

```
    Original string test string
    Test string after string n set # # # #   string
```

6. strtok():
- strtok function is used for splitting a string by some delimiter.
- For example we have comma separated list of items from a file and we want individual items in an array.
- Function splits string according to given delimiter and returns next token.
- It needs in a loop to get all tokens.

  Syntax: `char *strtok(char str[], const char * delims);`

7. strcmpic():
- str(mpic) function is same as strcmp() function. But this function negotiates case.
- In strcmpi "A" and "a" are treated same characters, where as strmp() function treats "A" & "a" as different character.
- It's a non-standard function which may not be available in standard library in C.
- strmpi() and strcmp() compass two given strings and returns zero if they are same.
- If length of string1 < string 2 it return <0 value.
- If length of string1 > string2 it returns > 0 value.

  Syntax: `int strcmpi(const char *str1, const char * str2);`

Program 3.15: Program to show use of strcmpi().

```c
#include<stdio.h>
#include<string.h>
main()
{
    char str1[] = "fresh";
    char str2[] = "refresh";
    int i, j, k;
    i = strcmpi(str1, "fresh");
    j = strcmpi(str1, str2);
    k = strcmpi(str1, "f");
    printf("\n % d % d %d", i, j, k);
}
```

Output:
```
0    -1    1
```

Program 3.16: Program by using strok() function.

```c
#include<stdio.h>
#include<string.h>
void main()
{
    char str[] = "NIRALI_PUBLICATION";
    char *token = strtok(str, "_");
    while(token! = NULL)
    {
        printf("%s \n"; token);
        token=strtok(NULL,"-");
    }
}
```

Output:
```
NIRALI
PUBLICATION
```

8. strrev() Function:

- This function reserves all the characters of a string except the terminating null character.

  Syntax: `char * strrev(char * str);`

Program 3.17: Program using strrev() library function.

```c
#include<stdio.h>
#include<string.h>
void main()
{
    char str[30];
    clrscr();
    puts("\nEnter a string:");
    gets(str);
    strrev(str);
    puts("After reversal the string is:");
    puts(str);
}
```

Output:

9. strlwr() Function:

- This function converts all the letters in a string to lowercase.

  Syntax: `char * strlwr (char * str);`

Program 3.18: Program using strlwr() library function.

```c
#include<stdio.h>
#include<string.h>
void main()
{
    char str[30];
    clrscr();
    puts("\nEnter a string:");
    gets(str);
    strlwr(str);
    puts("Lowercase string is:");
    puts(str);
}
```

Output:

```
C:\ TC

Enter a string:
NIRALI
Lowercase string is:
nirali
```

10. strupr() Function:

- This function converts all the letters in a string to uppercase.

  Syntax: `char* strupr (char* str);`

Program 3.19: Program using strupr() library function.

```c
#include<stdio.h>
#include<string.h>
void main()
{
    char str[30];
    clrscr();
    puts("\nEnter a string:");
    gets(str);
    strupr(str);
    puts("Uppercase string is:");
    puts(str);
}
```

Output:

```
C:\ TC

Enter a string:
science
Uppercase string is:
SCIENCE
```

11. strchr() Function:

- This function scans a string for the first occurrence of a given character.

  Syntax: `char * strchr (const char * str, int c);`

Program 3.20: Program using strchr() library function.

```c
#include<stdio.h>
#include<string.h>
void main()
{
    char str[30],ch;
    char* ptr;
    puts("\nEnter a string:");
    gets(str);
    puts("Enter a character to be found:");
    scanf("%c",&ch);
```

```
        ptr=strchr(str,ch);
        if(ptr==NULL)
            puts("Character not found");
        else
            printf("Character Found ");
    }
```

Output:

```
Enter a string:
Computer
Enter a character to be found:
a
Character not found
```

12. strrchr() Function:

- This function locates the last occurrence of a character in a given string.

    Syntax: `char * strrchr (const char * str, int c);`

Program 3.21: Program using strrchr() library function.

```
#include<stdio.h>
#include<string.h>
void main()
{
    char str[30],ch;
    char* ptr;
    puts("\nEnter a string:");
    gets(str);
    puts("Enter a character to be found:");
    scanf("%c",&ch);
    ptr=strrchr(str,ch);
    if(ptr==NULL)
        puts("Character Not Found");
    else
        printf("Character Found ");
}
```

Output:

```
Enter a string:
Nirali
Enter a character to be found:
r
Character Found
```

13. strstr() Function:

- This function finds the first occurrence of a string in another string.

    Syntax: `char * strstr (const char * str1, const char str 2);`

Program 3.22: Program using strstr() library function.

```c
#include<stdio.h>
#include<string.h>
void main()
{
    char* ptr;
    char str1[30];
    char str2[30];
    puts("\nEnter a string:");
    gets(str1);
    puts("Enter the string to be found:");
    gets(str2);
    ptr=strstr(str1,str2);
    if(ptr==NULL)
        puts("String not found");
    else
    {
        printf("Found in %s",ptr);
    }
}
```

Output:

```
Enter a string:
Ramayana
Enter the string to be found:
Ram
Found in Ramayana
```

14. strncpy() Function:

- This function copies at the most n characters of a source string to the destination string.

  Syntax: `char * strncpy (char * dest, const char * src, int n);`

Program 3.23: Program using strncpy() library function.

```c
#include<stdio.h>
#include<string.h>
void main()
{
    char src[60];
    char dest[60];
    int n;
    puts("\nEnter source strsing:");
    gets(src);
    puts("Enter the value of n:");
    scanf("%d",&n);
```

```
    puts("Source string is:");
    puts(src);
    strncpy(dest,src,n);
    dest[n]='\0';
    puts("Destination string is:");
    puts(dest);
}
```
Output:
```
Enter source string:
Nirali
Enter the value of n:
2
Source string is:
Nirali
Destination string is:
Ni
```

15. strncat() Function:

- This function concatenates a portion of one string with another. It also appends at the most n characters of a source string to a destination string.

    Syntax: `char * strncat (char * dest, const char * src, int n);`

Program 3.24: Program using strncat() library function.
```
#include<stdio.h>
#include<string.h>
void main()
{
    char dest[60];
    char src[60];
    int n;
    puts("\nEnter strings:");
    gets(dest);
    gets(src);
    puts("Enter the value of n:");
    scanf("%d",&n);
    puts("The strings are:");
    puts(dest);
    puts(src);
    strncat(dest,src,n);
    puts("After concatenation:");
    puts(dest);
}
```

Output:

```
Enter strings:
Nirali
Prakashan
Enter the value of n:
7
The strings are:
Nirali
Prakashan
After concatenation:
NiraliPrakash
```

16. strncmp() Function:

- This function compares a portion of two strings.

  Syntax: `int strncmp(const char * str1, const char* str2, int n);`

Program 3.25: Program using strncmp() library function.

```c
#include<stdio.h>
#include<string.h>
void main()
{
    char str1[30],str2[30];
    int res,n;
    puts("\nEnter string 1:");
    gets(str1);
    puts("Enter string 2:");
    gets(str2);
    puts("Enter the value of n:");
    scanf("%d",&n);
    res=strncmp(str1,str2,n);
    if(res==0)
        puts("Strings portions are equal");
    else
        puts("Strings portions are not equal");
}
```

Output:

```
Enter string 1:
Ramayan
Enter string 2:
Ram
Enter the value of n:
3
Strings portions are equal
```

17. strncmpi() Function:

- This function compares a portion of two strings without case sensitivity.

  Syntax: int strncmpi (const char * str1, const char * str2, int n);

Program 3.26: Program using strncmpi() library function.

```c
#include<stdio.h>
#include<string.h>
void main()
{
    char str1[20],str2[20];
    int res,n;
    clrscr();
    puts("\nEnter string 1:");
    gets(str1);
    puts("Enter string 2:");
    gets(str2);
    puts("Enter the value of n:");
    scanf("%d",&n);
    res=strncmpi(str1,str2,n);
    if(res==0)
        puts("Strings portions are equal");
    else
        puts("Strings portions are not equal");
}
```

Output:

3.9 COMMAND LINE ARGUMENTS - argc AND argv

- Command line argument is a parameter supplied to a program when program is invoked.
- With this two parameters/arguments are passed one in argc and second is argv.
- argc is an argument counter i.e. it counts number of arguments on command line.
- argv is an argument vector and represents an array of character pointers that points to command line arguments.
- The size of array will be equal to value of argc.

  Example: c:> program FILE1, FILE2, FILE3.

- There are four parameters supplied on command line. So argc = 4.

- argv is an array of four pointers to strings as below:

```
argv[0] = program
argv[1] = FILE1
argv[2] = FILE2
argv[3] = FILE3
```

- To access command line arguments declare main function with argc and argv parameters.

  Syntax:

```
main(int argc, char *argv[])
{


}
```

- Always first parameter in command line is program name so argv[0] is always program name. So argv[0] is always program name.

Program 3.27: Program for command line argument.

```c
#include <stdio.h>
#include <stdlib.h>
int main(int argc, char *argv[])   //  command line arguments
{
    if(argc!=5)
    {
        printf("Arguments passed through command line not equal to 5");
        return 1;
    }
    printf("\n Program name : %s \n", argv[0]);
    printf("1st arg : %s \n", argv[1]);
    printf("2nd arg : %s \n", argv[2]);
    printf("3rd arg : %s \n", argv[3]);
    printf("4th arg : %s \n", argv[4]);
    printf("5th arg : %s \n", argv[5]);
    return 0;
}
```

Output:

```
Program name: test
1st arg: this
2nd arg: is
3rd arg: a
4th arg: program
5th arg: (null)
```

Summary

- Character constants are enclosed in single quotes and string constants are enclosed in double quotes.
- Allocate sufficient space in a character array to hold the null character at the end.
- Using the address operator and with a string variable in the scanf function call is an error.
- It is a compile time error to assign a string to a character variable.
- Using a string variable name on the left of the assignment operator is illegal.
- When accessing individual characters in a string variable, it is logical error to access outside the array bounds.
- Strings cannot be manipulated with operators. Use string functions.
- Do not use string functions on array char type that is not terminated with the null character.
- Do not forget to append the null character to the target string when the number of characters copied is less than or equal to the source string.
- Be aware the return values where using the functions strcmp and strncmp for comparing strings.
- When using string functions for copying and concatenating strings, make sure that the target string has enough space to store the resulting string. Otherwise memory overwriting may occur.
- The header file<stdio.h> is required when using standard I/O functions.
- The header file <ctype.h> is required when using character handling functions.
- The header file <stdlib.h> is required when using general utility functions.
- The header file<string.h> is required when using string manipulation functions.

Check Your Understanding

1. While reading a string with scanf function it automatically inserts terminating null character.
   (a) True   (b) False
2. When initializing a string variable during its declaration we must include the nul character as part of string constant like "Hello \0".
   (a) True   (b) False
3. String variables cannot be used with assignment operator.
   (a) True   (b) False
4. We cannot perform arithmetic operation on character variables.
   (a) True   (b) False
5. gets function automatically appends the null character at the end of string read from the keyboard.
   (a) True   (b) False
6. The function getchar skips white space during input.
   (a) True   (b) False

7. The function call strcpy (s_2, s_1); copies string s_2 into string s_1.
   - (a) True
   - (b) False
8. String the function call strcmp("abc", "ABC"); returns positive number.
   - (a) True
   - (b) False
9. The function ____ is used to determine the length of a string.
   - (a) strcpy
   - (b) strlen
   - (c) strcmp
   - (d) strcat
10. Function call strcat (s_2, s_1), appends ____ to ______.
   - (a) s1, s2
   - (b) s2, s1
   - (c) none of the above
11. Function call strnset is used for ______.
   - (a) set of the portion of characters in string
   - (b) concate two strings
   - (c) copy one string to another
   - (d) splitting string by some delimiter
12. The function strncat has ______ parameters.
   - (a) 1
   - (b) 2
   - (c) 3
   - (d) 4
13. Command line arguments uses two parameters ______ and ______.
   - (a) arg c, arg v
   - (b) strlen, strcat
   - (c) arg c, strcmp
   - (d) strcmpi, arg v

Answers

1. (a)	2. (b)	3. (b)	4. (b)	5. (a)	6. (b)	7. (b)	8. (a)	9. (b)	10. (a)
			11. (a)	12. (c)	13. (a)				

Trace The Output

1.
```c
main()
{
    char s[] = "c is good programming language";
    char m[40];
    puts(t);
}
```
2.
```c
main()
{
    char food[ ] = "tasty";
    char *pt;
    pt = food + strlen(food);
    while(--pt >= food)
    puts(pt);
}
```

3. printf("%d", strcmp("push", "PULL"));
4. Assuming the variable string contains "Nirali Prakashan is the best" determine what will be output of following program statements.

```
(i)   printf("%s", string);
(ii)  printf("%25.10 s", string);
(iii) printf("%s:, string[0]);
(iv)  for(i = 0; string[i] ! = '\0'; i++)
          printf("%c", string[i]);
(v)   for(i=0; string[i]! = '\0'; i++;)
          printf("%d", \n", string[i]);
(vi)  printf("%c", \n", string[10] + 5);
```

Practice Questions

Short Answer Questions:
1. What is pointer?
2. How to declare define and initialize strings.
3. What is format specifier for string?
4. What is string literal/constant.

Long Answer Questions:
1. How to read and write from and to console using different in-built functions like scanf, printf, gets, puts, getchar, putchar etc.
2. What is the importance of NULL character in string storage.
3. What is concept of strings and pointers and how to use them.
4. What is array of pointers how is useful.
5. What are different predefined functions.
6. What is its use and its syntax with example like strcat, strncnp, strlen, strcpy, etc.
7. What is command line arguments argc and argv.

Previous Exam Questions

Summer 2017

1. If the two strings are identical, then strcmp() function returns: [1]

    (a) −1   (b) data and a link

    (c) 0   (d) yes

Ans. **(c)**

2. What is the difference between string variable and string literal?   [1]

Ans. Refer to Section 3.2.4.

3. Write syntax and prototype of the following functions: [4]

    (i)   strlen()   (ii) strcpy()

    (iii) strcat()   (iv) strcmp()

Ans. Refer to Section 3.9.

4. Write a C program to copy one string into another string (Copy alternate characters) **[3]**

   ```
   S1 = "Hello"
   S2 = "HlO"
   ```

Ans. Refer Program 3.8.

5. What are command line arguments? Write their advantages. **[4]**

Ans. Refer to Section 3.9.

6. C makes no difference between char S (10) and char *S. Comment. **[3]**

Ans. Refer to Section 3.2.

| Winter 2017 |

1. What will be the output of the program? **[1]**

```c
# include<stdio.h>
int main()
{
    char str1[] = "Hello";
    char star2[]= "Hello";
if(str1==str2)
    printf("equal\n");
else
    printf("unequal\n");
return 0;
}
```

   (a) equal   (b) unequal
   (c) error   (d) None of the above

Ans. **(b)**

2. What is the significance of argv[0]? **[1]**

Ans. Argv[0] contain the name of the program itself.

3. Write the prototype and usage of function strcat( ). **[1]**

Ans. Refer to Section 3.9.

4. Write a program to accept and display name of customer and search for a specific name using array of string. **[5]**

Ans. Refer to Section 3.6.

5. What is command line argument? Give advantages of command line argument. **[4]**

Ans. Refer to Section 3.9.

6. Write a user defined function to copy one string to another and return the copied string. **[3]**

Ans. Refer to Section 3.13.

7. Write a program to cheek whether the number is odd or even pass through command line argument. **[3]**

Ans. Refer to Section 3.9.

8. Write user defined function to convert a string to uppercase and return converted string. **[3]**

Ans. Refer to Section 3.11.

9. Write the prototype and syntax of the following: **[4]**

   (i)   strlwr( )   (ii) strchr( )

   (iii) strrev( )   (iv) strlen( )

Ans. Refer to Section 3.13.

10. Write a C program for accepting 2 number as command line argument find sum and difference of there number. **[3]**

Ans. Refer to Section 3.9.

Summer 2018

1. ______ symbol is used to terminate a string. **[1]**

   (a)   Null   (b)   \0

   (c)   •   (d)   /0

Ans. **(b)**

2. Trace the output. **[1]**

```
char str[20] = "Bye";
printf ("% C", * srt);
```

   (a)   Bye   (b)   B

   (c)   y   (d)   Error

Ans. **(b)**

3. Which of the following is appropriate for reading multi-word string? **[1]**

   (a)   printf()   (b)   scanf()

   (c)   gets()   (d)   puts()

Ans. **(c)**

4. What is purpose of strtok( ) Function? **[1]**

Ans. Refer to Section 3.13.

5. What is significance of argv[0]? **[1]**

Ans. Argv[0] contain the name of the program itself.

6. Write a C program that accepts 'n' words and display the longest word. **[5]**

Ans. Refer to Section 3.13.

7. Write a C program to check whether a string is palindrome or not. **[4]**

Ans. Refer to Section 3.13.

8. List any three string handling function with their usage. **[3]**

Ans. Refer to Section 3.13.

9. Write user defined functions to copy one string into another string and reverse the string without using standard library functions. **[5]**

Ans. Refer to Program 3.10.

■■■

4... Structures

Objectives...

- ■ To study definition, declaration, and initialization of structure.
- ■ To learn array of structure.
- ■ To study pointers to structure.
- ■ To study structures and functions.

4.1 INTRODUCTION

- A structure is a collection of variables of different data types under a single name.
- A structure is a convenient way of grouping several pieces of related information together.
- Unlike arrays, it can be used for the storage of heterogeneous data (i.e., data of different types).
- A structure is defined as, "a collection of elements of either same or different data type referred to by a common name". The various elements of a structure are known as members (also known as fields) of a structure.

4.2 CONCEPTS

4.2.1 Defining of Structure

- The definition of a structure informs the 'C' compiler about the type and the number of the data members forming the structure.
- A structure can be defined in C language by the keyword struct followed by its name and a body enclosed in curly braces. The body of the structure contains the definition of its members and each member must have a name. The declaration ends by a semicolon (;).
- The syntax for defining a structure is,

```
struct [structure_tag]
{
    member definition 1;
    member definition 2;
    . . . . . . . .

    . . . . . . . .
    member definition n;
} [one or more structure variables];
```

(4.1)

- **Example:** In following example, the struct Book declares a structure to hold the details of book which consists of three data fields, namely name, price and pages. These fields are called structure elements or members. Each member can have different data type, like in this case, name is of char type and price is of int type etc., Book is the name of the structure and is called structure tag.

```c
struct Book
{
    char name[20];
    int price;
    int pages;
};
```

Program 4.1: This program is used to store and access "id, name and percentage" for one student using structure. We can also store and access these data for many students using array of structures.

```c
#include<stdio.h>
#include<string.h>
struct student
{
    int id;
    char name[20];
    float percentage;
};
int main()
{
    struct student record = {0}; //Initializing to null
    record.id=11;
    strcpy(record.name,"Ajit");
    record.percentage = 72.5;
    printf("\nId is: %d \n", record.id);
    printf("Name is: %s \n", record.name);
    printf("Percentage is: %f \n", record.percentage);
    return 0;
}
```

Output:

```
Id is: 11
Name is: Ajit
Percentage is: 72.500000
```

4.2.2 Declaring Structure Variables

- To use a structure in a program efficiently, a structure variable needs to be declared. Structure variables are variables.

- It is possible to declare variables of a structure, after the structure is defined. Structure variable declaration is similar to the declaration of variables of any other data types.

- The syntax for declaring a structure variable is:

```
struct structure_name structure_variable;
```

- Structure variables can be declared in following two ways:

1. **Declaring Structure Variables Separately:**

```
struct Student
{
    char[20] name; int age;
    int rollno;
};
struct Student S1 , S2;        //declaring variables of Student
```

2. **Declaring Structure Variables with Structure Definition:**

```
struct Student
{
    char[20] name; int age;
    int rollno;
} S1, S2 ;
```

- Here, S1 and S2 are variables of structure Student. However this approach is not much recommended.

`4.2.3` Initialization of Structure

- A structure variable can be initialized in the similar manner to that of the initialization of any other data type variables.

- Like any other data type, structure variable can also be initialized at compile time.

- The general syntax of initializing structure variable is given below:

```
Storage_class struct tag variable={member_values separated by comma};
```

Example 1:

```
struct record
{
    char name[20];
    int 'roll_no';
    float marks;
} student = {"Deepali Bhoskar", 15, 92.50};
```

- The above structure variable declaration and initialization can also done in the following way,

```
struct record student=("Deepali Bhoskar", 15, 92.50);
```

Example 2:

```
struct Student
{
    float height;
    int weight;
    int age;
};
struct student sl = {180.75, 73, 23}; //initialization
```

Program 4.2: Program for student detail information.

```c
#include<stdio.h>
#include<conio.h>
void main()
{
    int num, i=0;
    /*Structure Declaration*/
    struct student
    {
        char name[20];
        int rollno;
        int t_marks;
    };
    struct student std[10];
    printf("\nEnter the number of students:");
    scanf("%d",&num);
    /*Reading student details*/
    for(i=0;i<num;i++)
    {
        printf("\nEnter the details for student %d",i+1);
        printf("\n\n Name");
        scanf("%s",std[i].name);
        printf("\n Roll No.");
        scanf("%d",&std[i].rollno);
        printf("\n Total Marks ");
        scanf("%d",&std[i].t_marks);
    }
    /*Displaying student details*/
    printf("\n Press any key to display the student details!");
    getch();
    for(i=0;i<num;i++)
        printf("\n student %d \n Name %s \n Roll No. %d \n Total Marks
        %d\n", i+1, std[i].name, std[i].rollno, std[i].t_marks);
    getch();
}
```

Output:

```
Enter the number of students:2
Enter the details for student 1
Name Sachin
Roll No.1
Total Marks 75
Enter the details for student 2
Name Nitin
Roll No.2
Total Marks 70
Press any key to display the student details!
student 1
Name Sachin
Roll No. 1
Total Marks 75
student 2
Name Nitin
Roll No. 2
Total Marks 70
```

4.2.4 Accessing Structure Members

- Once, a structure variable is declared and initialized, the individual structure members can be accessed with the help of dot operator (.).
- To access any member of a structure, we use the member access operator (.). The member access operator is coded as a period between the structure variable name and the structure member that we wish to access.
- The syntax for accessing the structure members is:

```
structure_variable.member_name
```

- To understand the concept of accessing structure members, consider following statements.

```
printf("%c",record11.grade);   /*displaying value of grade, the member of
                                 record1*/
record11.item_code=101;        /*assigning value to item_code of record11*/
```

Program 4.3: Program for accessing members of structure.

```c
#include<stdio.h>
#include<string.h>
struct Books
{
    char title[50];
    char author[50];
    char subject[100];
    int book_id;
};
```

```c
int main()
{
    struct Books Book1; /* Declare Book1 of type Book */
    struct Books Book2; /* Declare Book2 of type Book */

    /* book 1 specification */
    strcpy(Book1.title, "Advance C ");
    strcpy(Book1.author, "Deepali");
    strcpy(Book1.subject, "Basics of C Programming Tutorial");
    Book1.book_id = 3154;

    /* book 2 specification */
    strcpy(Book2.title, "C++");
    strcpy(Book2.author, "Atul");
    strcpy(Book2.subject, "C++ Tutorial");
    Book2.book_id = 2957;

    /* print Book1 info */
    printf("\nBook 1 title: %s\n", Book1.title);
    printf("Book 1 author: %s\n", Book1.author);
    printf("Book 1 subject: %s\n", Book1.subject);
    printf("Book 1 book_id: %d\n", Book1.book_id);

    /* print Book2 info */
    printf("Book 2 title: %s\n", Book2.title);
    printf("Book 2 author: %s\n", Book2.author);
    printf("Book 2 subject: %s\n", Book2.subject);
    printf("Book 2 book_id: %d\n", Book2.book_id);
    return 0;
}
```

Output:

```
Book 1 title: Advance C
Book 1 author: Deepali
Book 1 subject: Basics of C Programming Tutorial
Book 1 book_id: 3154
Book 2 title: C++
Book 2 author: Atul
Book 2 subject: C++ Tutorial
Book 2 book_id: 2957
```

4.3 ARRAY OF STRUCTURES

- A collection of similar types of structures is called an array of structures.
- The steps involved in creating an array of structures are as follows:

Step 1 : Declare a structure.

Step 2 : Then declare an array of structures using the following syntax:

```
struct<tag name><structure_variable> [size];
```

Step 3 : Suppose if the size specified is 10 then memory space is allocated for 10 different structures.

Step 4 : Similar to arrays, the arrays or a structure's index starts at 0.

Step 5 : The members of the array of structures are referred as follows:

```
<structure_variable_name> [index] . <member name>
```

- An array of structure is nothing but just a representation of structure variables as an array. For example, let us analyze a structure with structure_tag as class and student names, roll no and marks as the members of the tag class.
- Let us declare an array of students to represent the structure variables, such that each element of the array represents a structure variable.

```
struct class
{
    char name[20];
    int rollno;
    float marks;
};
struct class students[5];
```

- Here, the array with student as the array name, consisting of 5 elements (0 to 4 i.e., similar to array), is used to represent the structure variables such that each element is defined to be of the type struct class.
- This array of structure can be initialized in the following way:

```
struct class students[5] =    {
                              {"Amar",  01,   72.00}
                              {"Ram",   02,   66.50},
                              {"Prashant",    03,      60.00},
                              {"Gopal", 04,   63.50},
                              {"Hari",  05,   76.00},
                         };
```

Program 4.4: Program for array of structures.

```c
#include<stdio.h>
#include<string.h>
struct student
{
    int id;
    char name[30];
    float percentage;
};
```

```c
int main()
{
    int i;
    struct student record[2];
    // 1st student's record
    record[0].id=11,
    strcpy(record[0].name, "Ajay");
    record[0].percentage = 72.5;
    // 2nd student's record
    record[1].id=12;
    strcpy(record [1].name, "Prashant");
    record[1].percentage = 90.5;
    //3rd student's record
    record[2].id=13;
    strcpy(record[2].name, "Meenu");
    record[2].percentage = 81.5;
    for(i=0; i<3; i++)
    {
        printf("Records of STUDENT: %d \n", i+1);
        printf("Id is: %d \n", record[i].id);
        printf("Name is: %s \n", record[i].name);
        printf("Percentage is: %f\n\n",record[i].percentage);
    }
    return 0;
}
```

Output:

```
Records of STUDENT: 1
Id is: 11
Name is: Amar
Percentage is: 72.500000

Records of STUDENT: 2
Id is: 12
Name is: Prashant
Percentage is: 90.500000

Records of STUDENT: 3
Id is: 13
Name is: Meenu
Percentage is: 81.500000
```

4.4   POINTERS TO STRUCTURES

- Like we have array of integers, array of pointer etc., we can also have array of structure variables. And to make the use of array of structure variables efficient, we use pointers of structure type.
- Pointer which stores address of structure is called as pointer to structure.
- The pointers to structures have the following advantages:
  1. Passing a pointer to a structure as an argument to a function requires less data movement as compared to passing the structure to a function.
  2. It is simpler and easier to manipulate the pointers to structures than manipulating structures themselves.
  3. Some data structures (e.g. linked lists, trees, etc.) use the structures containing pointers to structures.

4.4.1   Declaring Pointer to a Structure

- The general syntax of declaring a pointer to a structure is:

```
[storage_class_specifier] [type_qualifier] struct named_structure type*
                                identifier_name={value 1, ... , value N};
```

- In the above syntax the terms enclosed within the square brackets are optional and might not be present in a declaration statement.

Program 4.5: Program for the declaration of a pointer to a structure.

```c
#include<stdio.h>
struct coord
{
    int x,y,z;
}
pt1={3,4,5},*ptr1;      /*Declaration of structure pointer at the time of
                                            structure definition */
void main()
{
    struct coord pt2={6,7,8};
    struct coord *ptr2=&pt2;   /*Declaration of structure pointer in a
                        separate declaration statement */
    ptr1=&pt1;
    printf("\nAddresses of pt1 and pt2 are %p%p\n",&pt1,&pt2);
    printf("Addresses of ptr1 and ptr2 are %p%p\n",&ptr1,&ptr2);
    printf("ptr1 and ptr2 point to %p%p\n",ptr1,ptr2);
    printf("Size of type(struct coord) is %d\n",sizeof(struct coord));
    printf("Size of type(struct coord*) is %d\n",sizeof(struct coord*));
    printf("pt1 and pt2 takes %d bytes\n",sizeof(pt1));
    printf("ptr1 and ptr2 take %d bytes\n",sizeof(ptr1));
}
```

Output:

```
Addresses of pt1 and pt2 are 0x6010400x7ffcb08ceef4
Addresses of ptr1 and ptr2 are 0x6010580x7ffcb08ceee8
ptr1 and ptr2 point to 0x6010400x7ffcb08ceef4
Size of type(struct coord) is 12
Size of type(struct coord*) is 8
pt1 and pt2 takes 12 bytes
ptr1 and ptr2 take 8 bytes
```

4.4.2 Accessing Structure Members via a Pointer to a Structure

- The members of a structure object in C language can be accessed via a pointer to a structure object by using one of the following two ways:
  1. By using the dereference or indirection operator (*) and the direct member access operator, and
  2. By using the indirect member access operator i.e., –> (arrow operator).
- The important points about accessing the structure members, via a pointer to the structure object are as given below:
  1. The general form to access a structure member via a pointer to the structure object using the dereference and dot operator is given below:

     ```
     (*pointer_to_structure_type).structure_member_name
     ```
  2. It is mandatory to parenthesize the dereference operator and the structure pointer because the dot operator has a higher precedence than the dereference operator.
  3. The members of a structure object can also be accessed via the pointer to the structure object by using only one operator, known as the arrow operator. The general syntax of such access is:

     ```
     pointer_to_structure_object–>structure_member_name
     ```

Program 4.6: Program for pointer to a structure.

```c
#include<stdio.h>
void main()
{
    struct student
    {
        char name[20];
        int m1, m2, m3;
    }*p,sink;
    int tot;
    p = &sink;
    printf("\nEnter student name:");
    scanf("%s",p->name);
    printf("Enter mark 1:");
    scanf("%d", &p->m1);
```

```
        printf("Enter mark 2:");
        scanf("%d", &p->m2);
        printf("Enter mark 3:");
        scanf("%d", &p->m3);
        tot = p->m1 + p->m2 + p->m3;
        printf("Total = %d", tot);
    }
```

Output:

```
Enter student name:Sourabh
Enter mark 1:45
Enter mark 2:75
Enter mark 3:68
Total = 188
```

4.5   STRUCTURES AND FUNCTIONS

- The C language supports passing structure as a arguments to the function.
- The three ways of passing a structure variable to a function in C language are as follows:
    1. Passing each member of a structure variable as a separate argument,
    2. Passing the entire structure variable by value, and
    3. Passing the structure variable by address/reference.

4.5.1   Passing Each Member of Structure as a Separate Argument

- A structure object in C language can be passed to a function by passing each member of the structure variable. The members of the structure variable can be passed by value or by address/reference.

Program 4.7: Program for passing of structure variables by the means of passing each of its members by value and by address/reference.

```
#include<stdio.h>
struct complex
{
    int re;
    int img;
};
void add_complex(int, int, int, int);
void mult_complex(int*, int*, int*, int*);
void main()
{
    struct complex no1,no2;
    printf("\nEnter the real and imaginary parts of 1st number:\t");
    scanf("%d%d",&no1.re,&no1.img);
    printf("Enter the real and imaginary parts of 2nd number:\t");
```

```c
        scanf("%d %d",&no2.re,&no2.img);
        add_complex(no1.re,no1.img,no2.re,no2.img);
        mult_complex(&no1.re,&no1.img,&no2.re,&no2.img);
}
void add_complex(int a, int b, int c, int d)
{
    if(b+d<0)
        printf("The result of their addition is %d%di\n",a+c,b+d);
    else
        printf("The result of their addition is %d+%di\n",a+c,b+d);
}
void mult_complex(int* a, int* b, int* c, int* d)
{
    int re,img;
    re=*a * *c;
    img=*a * *d+ *b * *c;
    if(img<0)
        printf("The result of their multiplication is %d%di\n",re,img);
    else
        printf("The result of their multiplication is %d+%di\n",re,img);
}
```

Output:

```
Enter the real and imaginary parts of 1st number:  1 3
Enter the real and imaginary parts of 2nd number:  2 3
The result of their addition is 3+6i
The result of their multiplication is 2+9i
```

4.5.2 Passing Structure by Value

- In C language, the member-by-member copy behavior of the assignment operator when applied on structures makes it possible to pass a structure variable to, and return a structure object from a function by value.

Program 4.8: In this program, the whole structure is passed to another function by value. It means the whole structure is passed to another function with all members and their values. So, this structure can be accessed from called function.

```c
#include<stdio.h>
#include<string.h>
struct student
{
    int id;
    char name[20];
    float percentage;
};
void func(struct student record);
```

```c
int main()
{
    struct student record;
    record.id=11;
    strcpy(record.name, "Prashant");
    record.percentage = 72.5;
    func(record);
    return 0;
}
void func(struct student record)
{
    printf("\nId is: %d \n", record.id);
    printf("Name is: %s \n", record.name);
    printf("Percentage is: %f \n", record.percentage);
}
```

Output:

```
Id is: 11
Name is: Prashant
Percentage is: 72.500000
```

4.5.3 Passing Structure by Address/Reference

- In C language, if the number of members in a structure variable is quite large, it is beneficial to pass the structure object by address/reference.
- This method of passing the structure object requires fixed data (i.e., equal to the size of a pointer) movement irrespective of the size of the structure object.

Program 4.9: In this program, the whole structure is passed to another function by address. It means only the address of the structure is passed to another function. The whole structure is not passed to another function with all members and their values. So, this structure can be accessed from called function by its address.

```c
#include<stdio.h>
#include<string.h>
struct student
{
    int id ;
    char name[20] ;
    float percentage;
};
void func(struct student *record);
int main()
{
    struct student rec;
```

```c
    rec.id=11;
    strcpy(rec.name, "Prashant");
    rec.percentage = 72.5;
    func(&rec);
    return 0;
}
void func(struct student *record)
{
    printf("\nId is: %d \n", record->id),
    printf("Name is: %s \n", record->name);
    printf("Percentage is: %f \n", record->percentage);
}
```

Output:

```
Id is: 11
Name is: Prashant
Percentage is: 72.500000
```

4.6 NESTED STRUCTURE

- Structure within structure is called nested structure. It means that a structure can also be user defined data type for member field of another structure.
- In other words, when a structure contains another structure, it is called nested structure.

   Syntax:

```c
    struct structurel
    {
        -----------------
        -----------------
    };
    Struct structure2
    {
        -----------------
        -----------------
        struct structure1 variable;
    };
```

   For example:

```c
    struct date
    {
        int day;
        char month [10];
        int year;
    }
```

```
struct person/*Outer structure declaration*/
{
    char name[20];
    int age;
    struct date dob;    /*Inner structure definition*/
};
struct person man;     /*Outer structure definition */
```

Program 4.10: Program for nested structure.

```c
#include<stdio.h>
struct Address
{
    char HouseNo[25];
    char City[25];
    char PinCode[25];
};
struct Employee
{
    int Id;
    char Name[25];
    float Salary;
    struct Address Add;
};
void main()
{
    int i;
    struct Employee E;
    printf("\nEnter Employee Id: ");
    scanf("%d",&E.Id);
    printf("\nEnter Employee Name: ");
    scanf("%s",&E.Name);
    printf("\nEnter Employee Salary: ");
    scanf("%f",&E.Salary);
    printf("\nEnter Employee House No: ");
    scanf("%s",&E.Add.HouseNo);
    printf("\nEnter Employee City: ");
    scanf("%s",&E.Add.City);
    printf("\nEnter Employee Pin Code: ");
    scanf("%s",&E.Add.PinCode);
    printf("\nDetails of Employees:");
    printf("\nEmployee Id: %d",E.Id);
    printf("\nEmployee Name: %s",E.Name);
```

```
    printf("\nEmployee Salary: %f",E.Salary);
    printf("\nEmployee House No: %s",E.Add.HouseNo);
    printf("\nEmployee City: %s",E.Add.City);
    printf("\nEmployee House No: %s",E.Add.PinCode);
}
```

Output:

```
Enter Employee Id: 111
Enter Employee Name: Prashant
Enter Employee Salary: 20000
Enter Employee House No: Alandi
Enter Employee City: Pune
Enter Employee Pin Code: 412201
Details of Employees:
Employee Id: 111
Employee Name: Prashant
Employee Salary: 20000.000000
Employee House No: Alandi
Employee City: Pune
Employee House No: 412201
```

4.7 typedef AND STRUCTURES

- By using typedef we can create new data type.
- The typedef in C language, feature is particularly convenient when defining structures, since it eliminates the need to repeatedly write struct tag whenever a structure is referenced. Hence, the structure can be referenced more concisely.
- Let us see how we can create user-defined structure using typedef. The general syntax of a user defined structure is given below:

```
typedef struct
{
    member 1;
    member 2;
       :
    member n;
} new type;
```

where, new-type is the user-defined structure type. Once, the structure is defined, the variables of structure type can be declared in terms of new data type.

```
typedef struct
{
    char id[10];
    char name[30];
    int rollno;
}student;
student s1, s2;
```

Note: Initially, the student is defined as a user defined data type. Then s1 and s2 are declared as structure variables of type student.

Program 4.11: Program for typedef with structure.

```c
#include<stdio.h>
#include<string.h>
typedef struct Books
{
    char title[50];
    char author[50];
    char subject[100];
    int book_id;
}Book;
int main()
{
    Book book;
    strcpy(book.title, "C Programming");
    strcpy(book.author, "Nilesh Jagtap");
    strcpy(book.subject, "C Programming Tutorial");
    book.book_id = 5407;
    printf("\nBook title: %s\n", book.title);
    printf("Book author: %s\n", book.author);
    printf("Book subject: %s\n", book.subject);
    printf("Book book_id: %d\n", book.book_id);
    return 0;
}
```
Output:
```
Book title: C Programming
Book author: Nilesh Jagtap
Book subject: C Programming Tutorial
Book book_id: 5407
```

Summary

- A structure is a collection of variables of different data types under a single name.
- A structure variable is declared and initialized, the individual structure members can be accessed with the help of dot operator (.).
- A collection of similar types of structures is called an array of structures.
- Pointer which stores address of structure is called as pointer to structure.
- The members of a structure object in C language can be accessed via a pointer to a structure object by using one of the following two ways:
    1. By using the dereference or indirection operator (*) and the direct member access operator, and
    2. By using the indirect member access operator i.e., –> (arrow operator).
- Structure within structure is called nested structure.
- The typedef in C language, feature is particularly convenient when defining structures, since it eliminates the need to repeatedly write struct tag whenever a structure is referenced. Hence, the structure can be referenced more concisely.

Check Your Understanding

1. Which of the following are themselves a collection of different data types?
   (a) String   (b) Structure
   (c) Char   (d) All of the mentioned
2. User-defined data type can be derived by _______.
   (a) struct   (b) enum
   (c) typedef   (d) All of the mentioned
3. Which operator connects the structure name to its member name?
   (a) –   (b) .
   (c) Both (b) and (c)
4. Which of the following cannot be a structure member?
   (a) Another structure   (b) Function
   (c) Array   (d) None of the mentioned
5. Which of the following structure declaration will throw an error?

   (a)
   ```
   struct temp{}s;
   main(){}
   ```
   (b)
   ```
   struct temp{};
   struct temp s;
   main(){}
   ```
   (c)
   ```
   struct temp s;
   struct temp{};
   main(){}
   ```
   (d) None of the mentioned

6. Number of bytes in memory taken by the below structure is?
   ```
   struct test
   {
   int k;
   char c;
   };
   ```
   (a) Multiple of integer size   (b) integer size+character size
   (c) Depends on the platform   (d) Multiple of word size
7. What is the output of this C code?
   ```
   void main()
   {
   struct student
   {
   int no;
   char name[20];
   };
   struct student s;
   s.no = 8;
   printf("%d", s.no);
   }
   ```
   (a) Nothing   (b) Compile time error
   (c) Junk   (d) 8

8. Point out the error in the program?

```
struct emp
{
    int ecode;
    struct emp e;
};
```

   (a) Error: in structure declaration
   (b) Linker Error
   (c) No Error
   (d) None of above

9. Which of the following operation is illegal in structures?
   (a) Typecasting of structure
   (b) Pointer to a variable of same structure
   (c) Dynamic allocation of memory for structure
   (d) All of the mentioned

10. A structure can be nested inside another structure.
   (a) True
   (b) False

Answers

1. (b)	2. (d)	3. (b)	4. (b)	5. (d)	6. (b)	7. (d)	8. (a)	9. (a)	10. (a)

Trace the Output

1.
```
int main()
{
    struct value
    {
        int bit1 : 1;
        int bit3 : 4;
        int bit4 : 4;
    } bit = {1, 2, 3};
    printf("%d, %d, %d \n", bit.bit1, bit.bit3, bit.bit4);
    return 0;
}
```

2.
```
struct student
{
    char name[20];
    int rollno;
}  s1, *ptr, n[10];
printf("\n %d", sizeof(s1));
printf("\n %d", sizeof(ptr));
printf("\n %d", sizeof(n));
```

```
3.  main()
    {
        struct
        {
            int i;
        } *ptr;
        (& * ptr)  → i = 10;
        pritnf("%d", ptr → i);
    }
4.  main()
    {
        struct a
        {
            int i;
        }
        struct a a;
        a·i = 100;
        printf("%d", a·i);
```

Practice Questions

Short Answer Questions:

1. What is structure.
2. What is nested structure.
3. How to access structure members.
4. How to declare pointer to structure.
5. What is mean by pointer to structure.

Long Answer Questions:

1. How to define a structure? Explain with example.
2. With the help of example describe structure declaration and initialization.
3. How to accessing members of structure? Explain with example.
4. Describe array of structures in detail.
5. What is bit field? Explain with program.
6. Explain pointers to structures in detail.
7. Write short note on: typedef and structures.
8. Define nested structure. Explain with example.
9. Explain structure and functions in detail.
10. What are the differences between typedef and #define.
11. Explain the following structure with example:
    (i)   Passing structure by value.
    (ii) Passing structure by address.
    (iii) Pointer to structure.

Previous Exam Questions

Summer 2017

1. Which of the following is a collection of different data types?
   (a) String   (b) Array
   (c) Structure   (d) Files
Ans. (c)

2. Define structure.
Ans. Refer to Section 4.2.1.

3. Write a program to accept details of n students (S_no, S_name, S_div, S_mark1, S_mark2) and display of 'A' division.   **[4]**
Ans. Refer Program 4.4.

4. Write a note on Array of structure.   **[3]**
Ans. Refer to Section 4.3.

5. What is a structure? How is a structure declared and initialized? Give an example.   **[5]**
Ans. Refer to Section 4.2.

6. How typedef can be used with structure.   **[3]**
Ans. Refer to Section 4.7.

Winter 2017

1. What is the similarity between a structure, union and enumeration?
   (a) All of them let you define new values.
   (b) All of them let you define new data type.
   (c) All of them let you define new pointers.
   (d) All of them let you define new structure.
Ans. (b)

2. Which of the following operations is illegal in structure?
   (a) Typecasting of structure
   (b) Pointer to a variable of same structure
   (c) Dynamic allocation of memory for structure
   (d) All of the mentioned
Ans. (a)

3. How the declaration of array of structure is done? Can it be initialized? Give an example.   **[4]**
Ans. Refer to Section 4.3.

4. Explain self-referential structure.   **[3]**
Ans. Self Referential structures are those structures that have one or more pointers which point to the same type of structures, as their member.

- Types of Self Referential structures:
  1. **Self Referential structure with single link:** These structures can have only one self-pointer as their member. E.g. singly
  2. **Self Referential structure with Multiple Links:** Self referential structures with multiple links can have more than one self pointers. E.g. doubly

5. Write a program to accept student data (rollno, name, marks) of 3 subjects. Calculate total percentage and average of each student and display class as per the percentage. **[5]**

Ans. Refer to Program 4.6.

Summer 2018

1. If variable is a pointer to a structure, then which of the following operator is used to access data members of the structure.

   (a) &　　　　　　　　　　　　　　　(b) •

   (c) *　　　　　　　　　　　　　　　(d) →

Ans. (d)

2. Find memory required for the following:

```
struct demo
{
    int x;
    char y [15];
} d;
```

[**Note:** Assume 'int' takes 4 bytes]

Ans. 19 bytes

3. Explain nested structure with an example. **[3]**

Ans. Refer to Section 4.6.

4. Write a C program to accept and display book details of 'n' books as book-title, author, publisher and cost. **[5]**

Ans. Refer to Program 4.4.

5. Trace the output and Justify **[3]**

```
struct student
{
    int roll ;
    char name [10];
} S1, * P, S[5];
printf ("% d % d % d", sizeof (S1), sizeof (P), sizeof(S));
```

Ans. 16 8 80

6. Explain 'pointer to structure' concept with example. **[4]**

Ans. Refer to Section 4.4.

∎∎∎

5... Advanced Features

Objectives...

- ■ To learn Efficient way of using the same memory location for multiple purposes.
- ■ To implement pseudo-polymorphism in C.
- ■ To learn reduce memory usage in bit-fields.

5.1 INTRODUCTION

- Union is the special form of structure, in which two or more variables share the same memory, but only one of them can be accessed at any moment.

- A union is a special data type available in C, that allows to store different data types in the same memory location. You can define a union with many members, but only one member can contain a value at any given time. Unions provide an efficient way of using the same memory location for multiple-purpose.

- A union can also be defined as, "a heterogeneous data type, defined by the user that group variables into a single entity".

- Union variables are the variables of union of type union tag and they can also be separately defined.

5.2 CONCEPT

- Union is a user define data type in C like Structure, that allows to store different data types in the same memory location.

- Unions provide an efficient way of using the same memory location for multiple-purpose.

- A union can also be defined as, "a heterogeneous data type, defined by the user that group variables into a single entity".

- A union is a variable that may hold objects of different types and size.

- Union provide a way to manipulate different kind of data in a single area of storage, without embedding any machine-dependent information in the program.

- Union may occur within structures and arrays, vice versa.

5.2.1 Declaration and Definition

- **Definition:** Union is a special datatype available in c, we use **union** keyword for defining a structure. In union all members are allocated in the same memory address. The union statement defines a new data type with more than one member for your program.
- Variables of a union type can be declared either at the time of union type definition or after union type definition in a separate declaration statement.
- Declaration of union must start with the keyword union followed by the union tag(name) and union's member variables are declared within braces.
- The format of the union statement is as follows:

Declaration:

Syntax:

```
union [union name]
{
    member definition;
    member definition;
        ...
    member definition;
} [one or more union variables];
```

- The union tag is optional and each member definition is a normal variable definition, such as int a; or float b; or any other valid variable definition. At the end of the union's definition, before the final semicolon, you can specify one or more union variables but it is optional.
- Here, is the way you would define a union type named Data having three members charVal, IntVal, FloatVal:

Example:

```
union Multiple
{
    char charVal;
    int  IntVal;
    float FloatVal;
};
```

Program 5.1: Program to display size of Union.

```
#include<stdio.h>
union Multiple
{
    char charVal;
    int  IntVal;
    float FloatVal;
};
```

```
int main()
{
    union Multiple m1;
    printf("\n Size of Union is %d ",sizeof(m1));
}
```

Output:
```
Size of Union is 4
```

5.3 INITIALIZATION AND ACCESSING UNION MEMBERS

- The members of a union variable share the same memory, the union variable can hold the value of only one of its member at a time. For this reason, while initializing a union variable, it is allowed to initialize its first member only.
- The variable values are called members of the union.
- To access any member of a union, we use the member access operator (.)
  Syntax: `union-name.member`

Program 5.2: To Initialization and Accessing Union member.

```
#include<stdio.h>
union variables
{
    char cval;
    int ival;
    float fval;
};
int main()
{
    union variables var;
    var.cval='K';
    printf("\ncharacter member is:%c",var.cval);
    var.ival=1200;
    printf("\nInteger member is:%i",var.ival);
    var.fval=13.4;
    printf("\nFloat member is:%f",var.fval);
    return 0;
}
```

Output:
```
character member is:K
Integer member is:1200
Float member is:13.400000
```

- Like structures, we can have pointers to unions and can access members using arrow operator (–>).
  Syntax: `union-point->member`

Program 5.3: Access members using arrow.

```c
#include<stdio.h>
union variables
{
    char cval;
    int ival;
    float fval;
};
void main()
{
    union variables var;
    var->cval='K';
    printf("The values of the members are value of cval =%c", var->cval);
    var->ival=840;
    printf("The values of the members are value of ival =%d", var->cval);
}
```

Output:

```
Character member is: K
Integer member is: 1200
Float member is: 13.400000
```

5.4　DIFFERNCE BETWEEN STRUCTURE AND UNION

- Following table differentiate Structure and Union.

Sr. No.	Structure	Union
1.	It is defined with 'struct' keyword.	It is defined with 'union' keyword.
2.	Structure allocates space for all its members separately.	Union allocates one common storage space for all its member.
3.	All members may be initialized.	Only its first member may be initialized.
4.	Structure members are stored at discrete locations in memory.	All the union members share common memory space.
5.	The size of a structure is equal to the sum of the sizes of its members.	The size of a union is equal to the size of its largest member.
6.	A structure is a user-defined data type which is a collection of an ordered group of data objects.	A union is also a user-defined type which is a collection of data objects that have different data types.
7.	Structures are not considered as memory efficient in comparison to unions.	Unions are considered as memory efficient in situations where the members are not required to be accessed simultaneously.

contd. ...

8.	We can access all members of structure at a time.	We can access only one member of union at a time.

9.	**Example:**
	struct student
	{
	int mark;
	char name[6];
	};
		Example:
		union student
		{
		int mark;
		char name[6];
		};

5.5 STRUCTURES WITHIN UNION

- As we know that structure and union are similar, and we can access structure within structure like that we can access structure in union.

Program 5.4: Program to access structure in Union.

```c
#include<stdio.h>
int main()
{
    struct student
    {
        char name[30];
        int rollno;
        float percentage;
    };
    union details
    {
        struct student st;
    };
    union details set;
    printf("\nEnter name: ");
    scanf("%s", set.st.name);
    printf("\nEnter roll no: ");
    scanf("%d", &set.st.rollno);
    printf("\nEnter percentage:");
    scanf("%f", &set.st.percentage);
    printf("\nThe student details are: \n");
    printf("\nName: %s", set.st.name);
    printf("\nRollno: %d", set.st.rollno);
    printf("\nPercentage: %f", set.st.percentage);
    return 0;
}
```

Output:

```
Enter name: Kamil
Enter roll no: 4001
Enter percentage: 80.40
The student details are:
Name:Kamil
Rollno: 4001
Percentage: 80.400000
```

5.6　UNION WITHIN STRUCTURES

- We can use a single structure for it but then it would lead to wastage of memory from union we use any one variable at a time. Both of them are never used simultaneously. So, here union inside structure can be used effectively:

Program 5.5: Program to access union within structure.

```c
#include<stdio.h>
struct student
{
    union
    { //union within structure
    char name[10];
    int roll;
    };
int mark;
};
int main()
{
    struct student stud;
    char choice;
    printf("\n You can enter your name or roll number ");
    printf("\n Do you want to enter the name (y or n): ");
    scanf("%c",&choice);
    if(choice=='y'||choice=='Y')
    {
        printf("\n Enter name: ");
        scanf("%s",stud.name);
        printf("\n Name:%s",stud.name);
    }
    else
    {
        printf("\n Enter roll number");
        scanf("%d",&stud.roll);
        printf("\n Roll:%d",stud.roll);
    }
```

```
        printf("\n Enter marks");
        scanf("%d",&stud.mark);
        printf("\n Marks:%d",stud.mark);
        return 0;
    }
```

Output:

```
You can enter your name or roll number
Do you want to enter the name (y or n): n
Enter roll number21
Roll: 21
Enter marks 45
Marks: 45
```

5.7 POINTERS AND UNIONS

- We know that pointer is special kind of variable which is capable of storing the address of another variable in c programming.

    Pointer to union: Pointer which stores address of union is called as pointer to union

```
        union team t1;       //Declaring union variable
        union team *sptr;    //Declaring union pointer variable
        sptr = &t1;          //Assigning address to union pointer
```

Program 5.6: Program for Pointers with union.

```c
#include<stdio.h>
union team
{
    char *name;
    int members;
    char captain[20];
};
int main()
{
    union team t1,*sptr = &t1;
    t1.name = "India";
    printf("\nTeam: %s",(*sptr).name);
    printf("\nTeam: %s",sptr->name);
    return 0;
}
```

Output:

```
Team = India
Team = India
```

5.8 NESTED UNIONS

- Unions can be nested, either with previously defined unions or with new internally defined unions. In the latter case the union names may not be necessary, but scoping rules still apply. (i.e. if a new union type is created inside another union, then the definition is only known within that union.)

Program 5.7: Program for nested union.

```c
#include <stdio.h>
union nested
{
    int a;
    union
    {
        int b;
    } ;
}s;
int main()
{
    printf("Enter Value for a and b");
    scanf("%d",&s.a);
    scanf("%d",&s.b);
    printf("Value of a is %d",s.a);
printf("Value of b is %d",s.b);
}
```

Output:

```
Enter Value for a and b
34 556
Value of a is 0.000000
Value of b is 556
```

- When we executing the above program that shows the only one value accepted by user because of union but it always showing the value of inner union which inside nested union.

5.9 ENUMERATED DATA TYPES

- Enumerated data types are a special form of integers, with the following constraints:
  - Only certain pre-determined values are allowed.
  - Each valid value is assigned a name, which is then normally used instead of integer values when working with this data type.
- Enumerated types, variables, and typedef, operate similarly to structs:

Syntax:

```c
enum flag{constant1, constant2, constant3, ....... };
enum week{Mon, Tue, Wed};
enum week day;
    or
enum week{Mon, Tue, Wed}day;
```

- Values may be assigned to specific enum value names.
  - Any names without assigned values will get one higher than the previous entry.
  - If the first name does not have an assigned value, it gets the value of zero.
  - It is even legal to assign the same value to more than one name.

Example:

```
enum Errors{ NONE=0, // Redundant.  The first one would be zero anyway
MINOR1=100, MINOR2, MINOR3, // 100, 101, and 102
MAJOR1=1000, MAJOR2, DIVIDE_BY_ZERO=1000}; // 1000, 1001 and 1000 again.
```

- Because enumerated data types are integers, they can be used anywhere integers are allowed. One of the best places in switch statements:

```
switch(nextMove ) {
case NORTH:
y++;
break;
// etc.
```

- The compiler will allow the use of ordinary integers with enumerated variables, e.g. trump = 2; , but it is bad practice.

Program 5.8: Program to display day using enumerated datatype

```
#include<stdio.h>
enum week{Mon, Tue, Wed, Thur, Fri, Sat, Sun};
int main()
{
    enum week day;
    day = Wed;
    printf("%d", day);
    return 0;
}
```

Output:

```
2
```

5.10   BIT FIELDS

- We can specify the size of structure and union members in bits.
- When it knows that only some bits would be used for a variable it reduces memory consumption.
- Bit fields allow efficient packaging of data in the memory.
- As we know, integer takes two bytes(16-bits) in memory. Some times we need to store value that takes less then 2-bytes. In such cases, there is wastages of memory.
- For example, if we use a variable temp to store value either 0 or 1. In this case only one bit of memory will be used rather then 16-bits. By using bit field, we can save lot of memory.

Why we need?

- The idea is to use memory efficiently when we know that the value of a field or group of fields will never exceed a limit or is withing a small range.

Syntax:

```
struct struct-name
{
    datatype var1: size of bits;
    datatype var2: size of bits;
    - - - - - - - - - -
    - - - - - - - - - -
    datatype varN: size of bits;
};
```

Program 5.9: Program for bit fields.

```c
#include <stdio.h>
#include <string.h>
/* define simple structure */
struct
{
    unsigned int widthValidated;
    unsigned int heightValidated;
} status1;
/* define a bit field structure */
struct
{
    unsigned int widthValidated: 1;
    unsigned int heightValidated: 1;
} status2;
int main()
{
    printf( "Memory size occupied by status1: %d\n", sizeof(status1));
    printf( "Memory size occupied by status2: %d\n", sizeof(status2));
    return 0;
}
```

Output:

```
Memory size occupied by status1: 8
Memory size occupied by status2: 4
```

- The bit field structure requires 4 bytes of memory space for status variable, but only 2 bits will be used to store the values.
- The simple structure requires 8 bytes of memory space but in actual, we are going to store either 0 or 1 in each of the variables. The C programming language offers a better way to utilize the memory space in such situations.

Program 5.10: Program to exceed more than 3 bits

```c
#include <stdio.h>
#include <string.h>
struct
{
    unsignedint age: 3;
} Age;
int main( )
{
    Age.age = 4;
    printf( "Sizeof( Age ): %d\n", sizeof(Age) );
    printf( "Age.age: %d\n", Age.age );
    Age.age = 7;
    printf( "Age.age: %d\n", Age.age );
    Age.age = 8;
    printf( "Age.age: %d\n", Age.age );
    return 0;
}
```

Output:

```
Sizeof( Age ): 4
Age.age: 4
Age.age: 7
Age.age: 0
```

5.10.1 Concept

- Members of structures can also be bit-fields. Bit-fields are integers which consist of a defined number of bits.
- A bit field is normally stored in a machine word that is a storage unit of length sizeof (int). The width of a bit field cannot be greater than that of a machine word.
- The declaration of a bit-field has the following form inside a structure:

```c
struct
{
    type [member_name]: width ;
};
```

- The variable elements of a bit field are discussed below:
  1. **type:** An integer type that determines how a bit-field's value is interpreted. The type may be int, signed int, or unsigned int.
  2. **member_name:** The name of the bit-field.
  3. **width:** The number of bits in the bit-field. The width must be less than or equal to the bit width of the specified type.

- The variables defined with a predefined width are called bit fields.
- A bit field can hold more than a single bit; for example, if you need a variable to store a value from 0 to 7, then you can define a bit field with a width of 3 bits as follows:

```
struct
{
    unsigned int age: 3;
} Age;
```

- The above structure definition instructs the C compiler that the age variable is going to use only 3 bits to store the value. If you try to use more than 3 bits, then it will not allow you to do so.

5.10.2 Need

- We have been using integer fields of size 16 bits to store data. There are occasions where data items require much less than 16 bits space. In such cases, we waste memory space.
- C language permits us to use small bit fields to hold data items and thereby to pack several data items in a word of memory. Bit fields allow direct manipulation of string of a string of preselected bits as if it represented an integral quantity.
- A bit field is a set of adjacent bit whose size can be from 1 to 16 bits in length. The data type is either int or unsigned int or signed int and the bit-length is the number of bits used for the specified name.
- Suppose your C program contains a number of TRUE/FALSE variables grouped in a structure called status, as follows:

```
    struct
    {
        unsigned int widthValidated;
        unsigned int heightValidated;
    } status;
```

- This structure requires 8 bytes of memory space but in actual, we are going to store either 0 or 1 in each of the variables. The C programming language offers a better way to utilize the memory space in such situations.
- If you are using such variables inside a structure then you can define the width of a variable which tells the C compiler that you are going to use only those number of bytes. For example, the above structure can be re-written as follows:

```
    struct
    {
        unsigned int widthValidated: 1;
        unsigned int heightValidated: 1;
    } status;
```

- The above structure requires 4 bytes of memory space for status variable, but only 2 bits will be used to store the values.

Advantages of Bit Fields:

1. The saving of storage space is considerably high when a large number of data is stored.
2. The storage space needed to store the details in a structure is reduced by using the bit fields.

Limitations of Bit Fields:

1. Bits fields cannot be accessed using a pointer.
2. We cannot obtain the address of bit fields and hence no input using scanf() function is permitted.
3. No array of bit fields is allowed in C language.
4. They cannot be declared static.
5. The sizeof operator cannot be used with bit fields.

`5.10.3` Uses

- Bit field can be used to reduce memory consumption when it is known that only some bits would be used for a variable. Bit fields allow efficient packaging of data in the memory.
- As we know, integer takes two bytes(16-bits) in memory. Some times we need to store value that takes less then 2-bytes. In such cases, there is wastages of memory. For example, if we use a variable temp to store value either 0 or 1. In this case only one bit of memory will be used rather then 16-bits. By using bit field, we can save lot of memory.

`5.11` MULTI-FILE PROGRAMS

- Multi-file programs are those programs where code is distributed into multiple files communicating with each other. This is a more practical and realistic approach towards advanced programming where we want loosely coupled code module that can communicate with each other.
- Programs contain many different functions, it is not convenient to place each function in an individual file, and then use the make utility to compile each file separately and link them together to produce an executable.
- Normally, small programs (100 lines of code or less) are done using one single file. However, large programs (specially, 1000 lines of code or larger) become quite unmanageable. This is due to periodic maintenance (adding, deleting and modifying features) and also for understanding what the program does. It is for these reasons that large programs need to break down into multiple files.

File categories

- In "C", most large programs are written using functions. Functions have:
  1. 'Functions' definitions are stored in function implementation file (or simply "implementation" file).
  2. Functions prototypes are stored in a header (or simply "include" file).
  3. The call to functions are stored in the file containing the main function call (main() reserved word). This file is generically referred to as "driver" file – since it "drives" all the functionalities.

- A large program may have one or more header file(s); one or more implementation file(s). However, it would ALWAYS have one and ONLY one "driver" file.
- An example: Assume you like to write a multi-file program with 2 functions "add" and "subtract". Here is how it would look like:

1. **addsub_header.h**

```
#include <stdio.h>
int add(int,int);
int sub(int,int);
```

2. **addsub_impl.c**

```
#include "addsub_header.h"
int add(int a, int b)
{
    return a+b;
}
int sub(int a, int b)
{
    return a-b;
}
```

```
For Compilation:
gcc -c addsub_impl.c
gcc -c addsub_driver.c
gcc addsub_impl.c addsub_driver.c
./a.out
```

3. **addsub_driver.c**

```
#include  "addsub_header.h"
int main()
{
    printf("%i",add(2,3));
    printf("%i",sub(9,4));
    return 0;
}
```

Programs

1. **Program for read member elements of union and display them.**

```
#include<stdio.h>
union student
{
    char name[32];
    float marks;
    int rno;
}s1;
```

```
    void main()
    {
        printf("\nEnter Name: ");
        gets(s1.name);
        printf("\nDisplaying: Name: %s",s1.name);
        printf("\nEnter Marks: ");
        scanf("%f",&s1.marks);
        printf("\nDisplaying: Marks: %.2f",s1.marks);
        printf("\nEnter RollNo: ");
        scanf("%d",&s1.rno);
        printf("\nDisplaying: RollNo: %d",s1.rno);
    }
```

Output:

```
    Enter Name: kamil khan
    Displaying: Name: kamil khan
    Enter Marks: 75
    Displaying: Marks: 75.00
    Enter RollNo:402
    Displaying:RollNo: 402
```

2. **Program declares a union consisting of batting average, bowling average, wickets taken.**

```
    #include<stdio.h>
    struct player
    {
        char name[20];
        union
        {
            float batavg,bowavg;
            int wickets;
        }stat;
    };
    void main()
    {
        struct player p1,p2,p3;
        strcpy(p1.name,"Virat");
        p1.stat.batavg=60;
        strcpy(p2.name,"Dhoni");
        p2.stat.bowavg=20.10;
        strcpy(p3.name,"Irfan");
```

```
    p3.stat.wickets=600;
    printf("\nThe Players Database is: ");
    printf("\n%s\t%f",p1.name,p1.stat.batavg);
    printf("\n%s\t%f",p2.name,p2.stat.bowavg);
    printf("\n%s\t%d",p3.name,p3.stat.wickets);
}
```

Output:

```
The Players Database is:
Virat  60.00
Dhoni  20.10
Irfan  600
```

3. **Program demonstrating union.**

```c
#include<stdio.h>
void main()
{
    union employee
    {
        int empno;
        char name[10];
        float salary;
    };
    union employee emp;
    printf("Enter EmpNo:");
    scanf("%d", &emp.empno);
    fflush(stdin);
    printf("Enter Emp Name:");
    scanf("%s",&emp.name);
    printf("Enter Emp Salary:");
    scanf("%f",&emp.salary);
    printf("Employee Information\n");
    printf("Name: %s \n",emp.name);
    printf("Salary; %f\n",emp.salary);
    printf("EmpNo: %d\n",emp.empno);
}
```

Output:

```
Enter EmpNo: 3
Enter EmpName: Kamil
Enter Emp Salary: 2000
Employee Information
Name:
Salary: 2000.000000
EmpNo: 1073741824
```

Note: Above output showing us only salary because of union only one member can be access at time.

4. Demonstration of Enum.

```c
#include<stdio.h>
enum year{Jan, Feb, Mar, Apr, May, Jun, Jul, Aug, Sep, Oct, Nov, Dec};
int main()
{
    int i;
    for (i=Jan; i<=Dec; i++)
    printf("%d ", i);
    return 0;
}
```

Output:

```
0 1 2 3 4 5 6 7 8 9 10 11
```

Summary

- Union is a user define data type in C like Structure, that allows to store different data types in the same memory location.
- Unions provide an efficient way of using the same memory location for multiple-purpose.
- A union can also be defined as, "a heterogeneous data type, defined by the user that group variables into a single entity".
- It is a special datatype available in C, we use union keyword in the same way as we did while defining a structure. In union all members are allocated in the same memory address. The union statement defines a new data type with more than one member for your program.
- We can specify the size of structure and union members in bits.
- When it knows that only some bits would be used for a variable it reduces memory consumption.
- Bit fields allow efficient packaging of data in the memory.
- Enumerated data types are a special form of integers, with the following constraints:
  - Only certain pre-determined values are allowed.
  - Each valid value is assigned a name, which is then normally used instead of integer values when working with this data type.
- Programs contain many different functions, it is not convenient to place each function in an individual file, and then use the make utility to compile each file separately and link them together to produce an executable.

Check Your Understanding

1. What is the similarity between a structure, union and enumeration?
   (a) All of them let you define new values
   (b) All of them let you define new data types
   (c) All of them let you define new pointers
   (d) All of them let you define new structures

2. User-defined data type can be derived by___________.
   (a) union   (b) enum
   (c) typedef   (d) All of the mentioned
3. Size of a union is determined by size of the.
   (a) First member in the union   (b) Last member in the union
   (c) Biggest member in the union   (d) Sum of the sizes of all members
4. Members of a union are accessed as________________.
   (a) union-name.member   (b) union-pointer->member
   (c) Both a & b   (d) None of the mentioned
5. Which of the following share a similarity in syntax?
   1. Union, 2. Structure, 3. Arrays and 4. Pointers
   (a) 3 and 4   (b) 1 and 2
   (c) 1 and 3   (d) 1, 3 and 4
6. Which of the following data types are accepted while declaring bit-fields?
   (a) char   (b) float
   (c) double   (d) None of the mentioned
7. Which of the following is not allowed?
   (a) Arrays of bit fields   (b) Pointers to bit fields
   (c) Functions returning bit fields   (d) None of the mentioned
8. Bit fields can only be declared as part of a structure.
   (a) False   (b) True
   (c) Nothing   (d) Varies
9. Bit fields CANNOT be used in union.
   (a) True   (b) False
10. The elements of union are always accessed using & operator
   (a) Yes   (b) No

Answers

1. (b)	2. (d)	3. (c)	4. (c)	5. (b)	6. (a)	7. (d)	8. (b)	9. (b)	10. (b)

Trace The Output

```c
1.  main()
    {
        enum days{MON=-1, TUE, WED=6, THU, FRI, SAT};
        printf("%d, %d, %d, %d, %d \n", MON, TUE, WED, THU, FRI, SAT);
        return 0;

    }
2.  main()
    {
        enum value{VAL1=0, VAL2, VAL3, VAL3, VAL3}Var;
        printf("%\n", sizeof(var)):
        return 0;

    }
```

```
3.  main(()
    {
        union a
        {
            int i;
            char ch[2];
        }
        union a, u;
        u·ch[0]=3;
        u·ch[1]=2;
        printf("%d, %d, %d \n", 4·ch[0], 4·ch[1], 4·i);
        return 0;
    }
```

Practice Questions

Short Answer Questions:
1. What is union?
2. What is nested union?
3. How to Declare union?
4. What is bitfield?
5. What is use of enum?

Long Answer Questions:
1. What is union? How to declare it? Explain with example.
2. How to accessing union members?
3. Compare structure and union with example.
4. What is bit field? How to declare it? Explain with example.
5. Explain Multifile program with example .
6. Explain Enumerated data type with example.
7. Write short note on:
   (i)   Nested union
   (ii)   Structures within union
   (iii) Union within structures
   (iv)   Pointers and unions,

Previous Exam Questions

Summer 2017

1. The size of union is size of the longest element in the union:
   (a) Yes   (b) No   [1]

Ans. **(a)**
2. All members of union can be accessed at a time–state true or false   [1]

Ans. False

  3. Explain how union can be used within structure.   **[4]**

Ans. Refer Chapter 6.

  4. Differentiate between structure and union   **[5]**

Ans. Refer to Section 5.4.

  5. How to declare a union and how their members can be accessed?   **[3]**

Ans. Refer to Sections 5.2 and 5.3.

Winter 2017

  1. What of the following comments about union is false?
- (a) Union is a structure whose members share same memory area
- (b) The compiler will keep track of what type of information is currently stored
- (c) Only one of the members of union can be assigned a value at particular time
- (d) Size allocated for union is the size of its member needing the maximum storage

Ans. **(b)**

  2. Define Union.

Ans. Refer to Section 5.1.

  3. "A union cannot be nested in a structure". State true/false.

Ans. False

  4. Define union and explain how union is used within a structure.   **[4]**

Ans. Refer to Sections 5.1 and 5.6.

Summer 2018

  1. How is a union declared?

Ans. Refer to Section 5.2.

  2. Write a difference between structure and union with example.   **[4]**

Ans. Refer to Section 5.4.

  3. Trace the output and Justify.   **[3]**

```c
union exam
{
    int a, b;
};
union exame;
e.a = 5;
e.b = 7
printf ("% d", e.a.);
```

Ans. If we consider syntax error then after e.b =7 semicolon required without considering any syntax error output is 7

  4. Define union. Explain how to access it's member. Give example.   **[3]**

Ans. Refer to Sections 5.1 and 5.3.

  5. Explain bitfield concept with an example.   **[4]**

Ans. Refer to Section 5.10.

■■■

6...

File Handling

Objectives...

- ▣ To Manipulate and Access data from Computer.
- ▣ To Perform Operations on File.
- ▣ To Examine the contents of File.
- ▣ To know Library functions.

6.1 INTRODUCTION

- A place from where we can reading data or writing data to is File. This includes disk files and it includes devices such as the printer or the monitor of a computer.

- C treats all information which access a program as though it were a stream of bytes: a file. The most commonly used file streams are stdin (the keyboard) and stdout (the screen), but more sophisticated programs need to be able to read or write to files which are found on a disk or to the printer etc.

- A program which reads data simply reads values from its file portal and does not have to worry about how they got there. This is extremely simple to work in practice. To use a file then, a program has to go through the following routine:

  (i) Open a file for reading or writing. (Reserve a portal and locate the file on disk or whatever.)

  (ii) Standard library functions are used to Read or write data for file handling.

  (iii) Close the file to free the operating system "portal" for use by another program or file.

  (iv) Files are divided basically in two types:

  (a) Stream-oriented (Standard or high-level), and

  (b) System-oriented (or low-level)

  (v) High level file I/O functions do their own buffer management whereas in low level file I/O functions buffer management has to be done by the programmer.

  (vi) A buffer is a block of memory where the data to be stored in file is placed temporarily.

6.2 | CONCEPT OF STREAM

- The I/O model does not distinguish between the types of physical devices supporting the I/O. Each source or sink of data (file) is treated in the same way, and is viewed as a **stream** of bytes.
- All C language I/O operations is done with streams.
- A stream is a sequence of bytes of data.
- C provides following streams:
  - (i) stdin: This is standard input stream, (opened for input).
  - (ii) stdout: This is a standard output stream, (opened for output).
  - (iii) stderr: This is a standard error stream, (opened for output)
- Different streams are used to represent different kinds of data flow. Each stream is associated with particular class, which contains member functions and definitions for dealing with that particular kind of data flow.
- A stream is accessed by a stream pointer as shown in Fig. 6.1. The stream pointer points to the beginning of a stream.
- A file is opened as a stream with the help of a pointer of type FILE. Having opened the file, it is accessed through a pointer in a fashion very similar to accessing an array of strings.

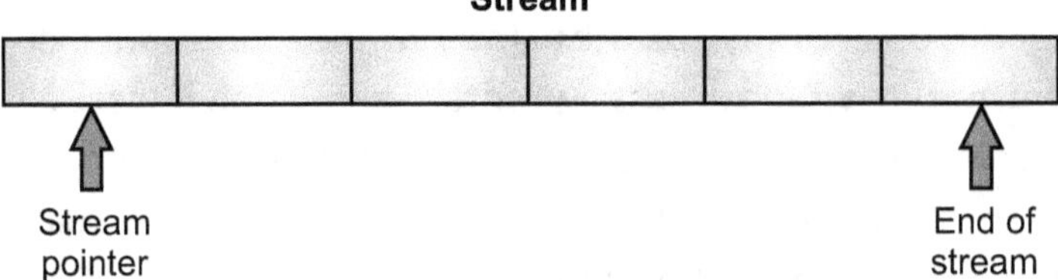

Fig. 6.1: Working of Streams

- There are two types of file, text files and binary files, which, within a program, are manipulated as text streams and binary streams once they have been opened for I/O. The stdio package does not permit operations on the contents of files 'directly'.

6.2.1 | Text Streams

- The Standard specifies what is meant by the term text stream, which essentially considers a file to contain lines of text? A line is a sequence of zero or more characters terminated by a newline character. It is quite possible that the actual representation of lines in the external environment is different from this and there may be transformations of the data stream on the way in and out of the program; a common requirement is to translate the '\n' line-terminator into the sequence '\r\n' on output, and do the reverse on input

6.2.1 | Binary Streams

- A binary stream is a sequence of characters that can be used to record a program's internal data, such as the contents of structures or arrays in binary form. Data read in from a binary stream will always compare equal to data written out earlier to the same stream, under the same implementation. In some circumstances, an implementation-defined number of NULL characters may be appended to a binary stream. The contents of binary files are exceedingly machine specific, and not, in general, portable.

6.2.3 Why files are needed?

- When a program is terminated, the entire data is lost. Storing in a file will preserve your data even if the program terminates.
- If you have to enter a large number of data, it will take a lot of time to enter them all.
- However, if you have a file containing all the data, you can easily access the contents of the file using few commands in C.
- You can easily move your data from one computer to another without any changes.

6.3 TYPES OF FILES

- There are two types of files:
  o Text files
  o Binary files

1. **Text files**
- Text files are the normal .txt files that you can easily create using Notepad or any simple text editors.
- When you open those files, you'll see all the contents within the file as plain text. You can easily edit or delete the contents.
- They take minimum effort to maintain, are easily readable, and provide least security and takes bigger storage space.

2. **Binary files**
- Binary files are mostly the .bin files in your computer.
- Instead of storing data in plain text, they store it in the binary form (0's and 1's).
- They can hold higher amount of data, are not readable easily and provides a better security than text files.

6.4 OPERATIONS ON FILE

6.4.1 Defining a File

- File is a collection of information stored in the secondary memory, having some filename, which is stored in the directory.

OR

- File is a set of instructions.
- File is not opening, before opening a file we need to establish a file pointer.
  FILE * fptr;
- FILE is a structure defined in the header file, "stdio.h".
- This header files stores all the information regarding the file i.e. name of the file, in what mode it is opened, starting buffer address, a character pointer which points to the character being read. The above statement establishes a buffer area. Each file opening has its own file structure. Before processing any file, it must be opened.

6.4.2 Opening a File

- On opening a file link is established between the program and the operating system through the FILE structure, since, operating system returns a pointer to the structure FILE.
- Opening a file associates the file name with buffer area. The fopen () function opens a file whose name is pointed to by 'filename' and returns the stream that is associated with it.
- The file opening function is written as:

  fopen (file-name, file-type);

  where, file-name= Name of data file to be opened

  file-type= Mode or manner in which data will be used
- The different modes in which the file can be opened are:

Mode	Meaning	Mode	Meaning
"r"	Open a text file for reading	"r + b"	Open a binary file for read/write
"w"	Create a text file for writing	"w + b"	Create a binary file for read/write
"a"	Append to a text file	"a + b"	Open or create binary file for read/write
"rb"	Open a binary file for reading	"rt"	Open a text file for reading
"wb"	Create a binary file for writing	"wt"	Create a text file for writing
"ab"	Append to a binary file	"at"	Append to a text file
"rt"	Open a text file for read/write	"r + t"	Open a text file for read/write
"wt"	Create a text file for read/write	"w + t"	Create a text file for read/write
"at"	Open or create a text file for read/write	"a + t"	Open or create a text file for read/write

- **Important points to remember while selecting modes:**
  1. When the mode is "writing (w)" a file with the specified name is created if the file does not exist. If the file already exists, the contents are deleted and the file is opened a fresh.
  2. When the purpose is 'appending', the file is opened with the current contents safe. A file with the specified name is created if the file does not exist.
  3. If the purpose is "reading", and if it exists then the file is opened with the current contents same. If the file does not exist, it creates an error.
  4. r + the existing file is opened to the beginning for both reading and writing.
  5. w + Same as w except both reading and writing.
  6. a + Same as a except both for reading and writing.

- From the above explanations, it is expected the above table would be clear.

  Examples:

  ```
  file *f1, *f2;
  f1 = fopen ("data", "w");
  f2 = fopen ("input", "r");
  ```

- We can open any number of files at a time.

6.4.3 Closing a File

- It is necessary that when in the program a file is opened then it should be closed as soon as the work with the file is over or atleast at the end of program.
- This ensures that all outstanding information associated with the file is flushed out from the buffers and all links to the file are broken. It also prevents any accidental misuse of the file. Also we have to close the file if we want to open the same file in a different mode.

  Syntax:

  ```
  fclose (file-pointer);
  ```
  OR
  ```
  fclose all();
  ```

  For example:

  ```
  FILE *p1, *p2;
  p1 = fopen ("input", "r");
  p2 = fopen ("output", "w");
  ________


  ________
  fclose (p1);
  fclose (p2);
  ```

- The syntax for closing the file is same, irrespective of the mode in which it is opened.

6.4.4 End of File (feof( ))

- Sometimes, we do not know how big the file is. To detect end of file we use feof();
- The function feof can be used to check the end-of-file condition on a file. Its prototype/ syntax is:

  ```
  int feof(FILE *fp);
  ```

- For example, to copy a file (associated with fp) to the standard output, we could use this statement:

  ```
  while(!feof(fp))
  putchar(getc(fp));
  ```

- In text files, a special character EOF denotes the end of file. End-of-File can be detected, as soon as this character is read. In binary files, the EOF is not there.
- feof function will not return true, and the program will be stuck in the loop. As a result, it is better to write the following (ch is an int):

  ```
  while((ch = fgetc(fp)) != EOF) putchar(ch);
  ```

- Now, if a file error is encountered, fgetc() will return EOF, and the loop will terminate

Syntax:

```
feof(file_pointer);
```

For example:

```
while (! feof (fptr))
{

    ______
    ______
    ______

}
```

Program 6.1: C program to illustrate how to file stored on the disk is read.

```c
#include<stdio.h>
#include<stdlib.h>
void main()
{
    FILE *ptr;
    char filename[15];
    char ch;
    printf("Enter the filename to be opened \n");
    scanf("%s", filename);/* open the file for reading */
    ptr = fopen(filename, "r");
    if(ptr == NULL)
    {
        printf("Cannot open file \n");
        exit(0);
    }
    ch = fgetc(ptr);
    while(ch!=EOF)
    {
        printf("%c", ch);
        ch = fgetc(ptr);
    }
    fclose(ptr);
}
```

6.5 RANDOM ACCESS TO FILES

- In the beginning we had considered about some functions. Now, we try to study and understand those functions one by one.

1. **ftell( ) Function:**

- This function just tells us the relative position of pointer (in bytes) i.e. number of bytes written in the file.

- This function tells where the pointer is positioned right now. It returns this pointer as a long integer which is an offset from the beginning of the file. returns – 1L on error
long ftell(FILE * fp);
For example: n = ftell (fp)
So fp is a file pointer and the value of bytes will be stored in n.n should be an integer.

Program 6.2: Program for ftell() function.

```c
#include<stdio.h>
void main()
{
    FILE *fp;
    char ch;
    long pos;
    clrscr();
    fp = fopen("file.txt","r"); //Statement 1
    if(fp == NULL)
    {
        printf("\nCan't open file or file doesn't exist.");
        exit(0);
    }
    printf("\nData in file...\n");
    while((ch = fgetc(fp))!=EOF) //Statement 2
    {
        if(ch=='a' || ch=='e' || ch=='i' || ch=='o' || ch=='u')
        {
            pos=ftell(fp);
            printf("\nPosition of %c is at %ld",ch,pos);
        }
    }
    fclose(fp);
}
```

Output:

```
Data in file...
Position of a is at 3
Position of i is at 15
```

2. rewind( ) Function:

- This function is used when the file is opened in append mode. This will again reset the pointer to the beginning of the file.
- This function places the pointer to the beginning of the file, irrespective of where it is present right now.

```c
void rewind(FILE * fp);
```

For example: rewind (fp)
where fp is a file pointer. So file pointer will be set to beginning of file.
For example: rewind(fp);
     n = ftell (fp);

- So n will be assigned a value 0. An important point to note, the first byte in file is numbered as 0, second as 1 and so on. This function helps us to read and write a file or read the file more than one, without having to close and open the file.

Program 6.3: Program of rewind() function.

```c
#include<stdio.h>
void main()
{
    FILE *fp;
    char ch;
    clrscr();
    fp = fopen("file.txt","a+"); //Statement 1
    if(fp == NULL)
    {
        printf("\nCan't open file or file doesn't exist.");
        exit(0);
    }
    printf("\nWrite some data:\n");
    while((ch=getchar())!='q') //Statement 2
    fputc(ch,fp);
    rewind(fp); //Statement 3
    printf("\nData in file:\n");
    while((ch = fgetc(fp))!=EOF) //Statement 4
    printf("%c",ch);
    fclose(fp);
}
```

Output:

```
Write some data:
hiq
Data in file
```

3. fseek( ) Function:

- With this function we can move the file pointer to a desired position.
- General format is:

```
fseek (file ptr, offset, position)
```

- where first parameter is the file pointer. Offset is number or variable of type long, and position is an int number. The offset specifies the number of positions (bytes) to be moved from the location specified by position. The position can have 3 values,

Macro name	Value	Meaning
SEEK_SET	0	Beginning of file
SEEK_CUR	1	Current position
SEER_END	2	End of file
For example:		

fseek(fptr, 0, SEEK_END); This positions the pointer to end of the line.

Program 6.4: Program for fetch record of student using fseek() function.

```c
#include<stdio.h>
struct Student
{
    int roll;
    char name[25];
    float marks;
};
void main()
{
    FILE *fp;
    char ch;
    int offset;
    struct Student Stu;
    clrscr();
    fp = fopen("Student.dat","r"); //Statement 1
    if(fp == NULL)
    {
        printf("\nCan't open file or file doesn't exist.");
        exit(0);
    }
    printf("\n\nLast record in file.\n");
    offset = sizeof(Stu)*-1;
    fseek(fp,offset,SEEK_END);
    fread(&Stu,sizeof(Stu),1,fp);
    printf("\n\tRoll: %d",Stu.roll);
    printf("\n\tName: %s",Stu.name);
    printf("\n\tMarks: %f",Stu.marks);
    printf("\n\nFirst record in file.\n");
    fseek(fp,0,SEEK_SET);
    fread(&Stu,sizeof(Stu),1,fp);
    printf("\n\tRoll: %d",Stu.roll);
```

```c
        printf("\n\tName: %s",Stu.name);
        printf("\n\tMarks: %f",Stu.marks);
        printf("\n\nSecond record in file.\n");
        fseek(fp,0,SEEK_CUR);
        fread(&Stu,sizeof(Stu),1,fp);
        printf("\n\tRoll: %d",Stu.roll);
        printf("\n\tName: %s",Stu.name);
        printf("\n\tMarks: %f",Stu.marks);
        fclose(fp);
    }
```

Output:

```
Last Record in File.
    Roll:1
    Name:kamil
    Marks:87.000000
Last Record in File.
    Roll:2
    Name:Ajmal
    Marks:86.000000
Last Record in File.
    Roll:3
    Name:adil
    Marks:80.000000
```

Program 6.5: Program to reverse a file using fseek().

```c
    #include<stdio.h>
    main()
    {
        typedef struct
        {
            char name[10];
            int emp_no;
            int salary;
        }record;
        record emp;
        FILE *fs, *ft;
        long recsize;
        int k, n;
        long lCurrentPos;
        int bIsEOF = 0;
        recsize = sizeof(emp);
```

```
fs = fopen("recordb.txt","r");
ft = fopen("recordbr.txt","w");
fseek(fs,-recsize,SEEK_END);
fseek(ft,0,SEEK_SET);
do
{
    k = fread (&emp,recsize, 1, fs);
    printf("\nKamil read= %d",k);
    n = fwrite(&emp,recsize, 1, ft);
    printf("\nN written = %d"n);
    lCurrentPos = ftell( fs );
    if ( lCurrentPos== recsize )
    {
        if ( bIsEOF )
        {
            /*All file is parsed reached at the end of record */ break;
        }
        fseek(fs, - (recsize), SEEK_cuR);
        /* This is last record which is going to write in the file so
        next loop we will break after writing this record for this make
        flag to true */
        bIsEOF = 1;
    }
    else
    {
        fseek(fs,- (2*recsize),SEEK_CUR);
    }
}while(lCurrentPos);
fclose(fs);
fclose(ft);
}
```

6.6 STANDARD LIBRARY FUNCTIONS FOR FILE HANDLING

- Before using any file it is necessary to create the file. It can be created by,
  1. Using any text editor directly, and
  2. By writing a program, to write into the file.
- Program will consist of accepting character input from user and writing to the file using file processing function 'fputc'. Any existing file or file created in the above manner can be read in any of the following way:
  1. Directly by using operating system commands, such as print or type.
  2. Using the text editor or word processor.
  3. A program can be written to read the file.

- In the program function fgetc( ) reads characters from data file and putchar( ) will display them on the screen. Individual data characters can also be processed as they are read.
- Thus, fputc() is a function used to write data character in a file.

```
intfputc (int ch, FILE *ptvar)
ch = character to be written
ptvar = File pointer
```

- fgetc() is the counterpart of the function fputc, and it is used to read a character from the file. It returns the character read to the calling program.

```
intfgetc (FILE * ptvar)
```

1. **getc( ) and putc( ) Functions:**
- These are the simplest input/output functions used for files. With these we can put in and get out a single character from a file.
- To use a putc function it is necessary that the file must be opened in writing mode. It is similar to puts( ) function. The fopen() function opens a file whose name is pointed to by 'filename' and returns the stream that is associated with it.
- The difference is that putc can only put a single character. The similarity is puts put a string on screen and putc( ) puts a character in file.
- The **general format of putc( )** is,

```
putc (c, fp1)
```

where c is a character and

```
fp1 is a file pointer.
```

- The fgetc() function returns the next character from the specified input stream and increments the file position indicator. The character is read as an unsigned char that is converted to an integer. If the end-of-file is reached, fgetc() returns EOF. If fgetc() encounters an error, EOF is also returned.
- The **general format of getc()**,

```
getc (fp2)
```

where, fp2 is a file pointer which is already opened in reading mode.
- When a file is opened the file pointer is set to the beginning of the file - when we perform certain operation in the file the pointer points to some variable address.
- Whereas, when a file is closed the compiler automatically puts a EOF mark. This determines the end of file. Again if the file is opened the pointer marks to the beginning of file.
- To stop inputting data or to close the file we can use ^z [control z] at the end of input. This will close the file.

Program 6.6: Program to demonstrate file input/output.

```
#include<stdio.h>
#include<conio.h>
void main()
{
    FILE *f1;
    char c;
    clrscr();
```

```
        printf("Data Input\n\n");
        f1 = fopen("INPUT", "w")
        while((c=getchar()) ! = EOF)
        putc(c, f1);
        fclose(f1);
        printf("\nData Output\n\n");
        f1 = fopen("INPUT", "r");
        while((c=getc(f1)) !=EOF)
        printf("%c", c);
        fclose(f1);
        getch():
    }
```

2. **getw( ) and putw( ) Functions:**

- These are similar to the getc( ) and putc( ) function. The only difference is with this we can read and write on integer or numeric quantity from the file.
- The **general formats** are:

```
    putw (integer, fp);
```

    And

```
    getw (fp);
```

    where, fp is the file pointer.

- For this purpose we choose 3 different files. In the first file first we store the list. We close the file and open it again in reading mode. At the same time we open two different files odd and even in writing mode.
- We read an int from first file and find whether it is even or odd. We put it in corresponding file. Then we close all the file and then open odd and even in reading mode. We just read the files and display the contents on screen.

Program 6.7: Program to demonstrate files.

```
#include<stdio.h>
#include<stdlib.h>
main()
{
    file *fp1, *fp2, *fp3;
    inti,no;
    clrscr();
    fp1=fopen("input","w");
    printf("please enter the list and enter - 1 to end:");
    do
    {
        scanf("%d",&no);
        if (no == -1)
```

```c
            break;
            else
            putw (no,fp1);
    }
    while(1);
    fclose(fp1);
    fp1=fopen("input","r");
    fp2=fopen("odd","w");
    fp3=fopen("even","w");
    do
    {
        no=getw(fp1);
        if(no==EOF)
        break;
        else
        {
            if(no%2==0)
            put(no,fp3);
            else
            putw(no,fp2);
        }
    }
    while(1);
    fcloseall();
    fp1=fopen("even","r");
    fp2=fopen("odd","r");
    printf("\nTHE EVEN NUMBERS ARE:");
    do
    {
        no=getw(fp1);
        if(no==EOF)
        break;
        else
        printf("\n%d",no);
    }
    while(1); fclose(fp1);
    printf("\nTHE CONTENTS OF ODD FILE ARE:"); do
    {
        no=getw(fp2);
        if(no==EOF)
        break; else printf("%\nd",no);
    }
    while(1);
    fcloseall();
    getch();
}
```

Output:

```
Please enter the list and enter - 1 to end:
    12345678910-1
The constants of even file are
    2
    4
    6
    8
    10
The contents of odd file are
    1
    3
    5
    7
    9
```

- So we have demonstrated a programme which utilizes file functions.

3. **fprintf( ) and fscanf( ) Functions:**

- These are similar to printf( ) and scanf( ) functions in a single way.

    (i)   **printf( ):** function writes on the screen and fprintf( ) writes in the file.

    (ii) **scanf( ):** function reads from the standard i/p device and fscanf( ) reads data from the file.

- The fprintf() function outputs the values of the arguments that makes up the argument list as specified in the format string to the stream pointed to by stream. The operations of the format control string and command are identical to those in printf().

- The **general format of fprint** is,

```
    i.e. fprintf (fp, "control string", list)
```

OR

```
    fprintf (pointer name, "control string", argument)
```

where fp is the file pointer. The control string contains output specifications for the items in the list. The list may include variables constants and strings.

```
    fprintf (fp1, "%d %s %d", mark,s name, roll);
```

- The fscanf function works exactly like the scanf function except that it reads the information from the stream specified by stream instead of standard input device.

- The **general format of fscanf function is,**

```
    i.e. fscanf(fp, "control string", list);
```

OR

```
    fscanf(ptr, "control string", list);
```

- This will read elements from the file specified by the pointer fp, according to specifications contained in the control string.

For example:

```
fscanf (fp, "%s %d", name, &phno);
```

These functions are much comparable to the ordinary printf and scanf functions. If the end of file is reached, fscanf () returns a EOF value.

With the functions in order to put input or get output from a file we have to use functions stdin and stdout we will consider the explanation after the following example.

Program 6.8: Program to demonstrate fprintf() and fscanf() functions.

```
#include<stdio.h>
#include<stdlib.h>
main()
{
    FILE *fp1
    int phno,wt,ht,n,i;
    char name[30], filename[20];
    printf ("Input filename");
    scanf ("%s", filename);
    fp1 = fopen (filename, "w");
    printf ("How many no. of i/p:");
    scanf("%d", &n);
    for(i=0;i<n; i ++)
    {
        fscanf (stdin, "%s %d %d", name, &phno, &wt, &ht);
        fprintf (fp1, "%s %d %d", name, phno, wt, ht);
    }
    fclose (fp1);
    printf ("\n \n");
    fp1 = fopen (filename, "r");
    printf ("\n Name \t phno \t wt \t ht");
    for(i=0;i<n;i++)
        {
            fscanf (fp1, "%s %d %d %d", name, &phno, &wt, &ht);
            fprintf (stdout, "%s \t %d \t %d \t %d, name, phno, wt, ht);
        }
        fclose all ();
    }
    /* end of main */
```

Output:

```
Input file name:
Mangala stores.
How many number of records in i/p: 2
Deepak 62119  60 5.8
Sachin 459520 62 5.7
```

- Now whatever is to be written in file is gives form the keyboard. Data is read using the function fscanf ( ) from the file stdin, which refers to the terminal and then it is written to the file pointed by the file pointer fp1.
- When the file is opened in reading mode, the data from the file along with the item values are written to the file stdout, which refers to the screen. While reading from a file care should be taken to use the same format specification with which the constants have been written to the file.

4. **fgets( ) and fputs( ) Functions:**

- These are similar to the gets( ) and puts( ) function. These functions are useful to input and output strings from the file.
- The fgets() function reads up to num-1character from stream and store them into a character array pointed to by str. Characters are read until either a newline or an EOF is received or until the specified limit is reached. After the character has been read, a null is stored in the array immediately after the last character is read. A newline character will be retained and will be a part of the array pointed to by str.
- If successful, fgets() returns str; a null pointer is returned upon failure. If a read error occurs, the content of the array pointed to by str are indeterminate.
- The **standard format for fgets()** is:

```
fputs(cont char *str, file *fp)
```

i.e.

```
fputs(string to be inputted, file pointer)
```

- The fputs() function writes the content of the string pointed to by str to the specified stream. The null terminator is not written. The fputs() function returns non negative on success and EOF on failure.
- The **format for fputs()** is:

```
fgets (char *str, int length, file *fp)
```

i.e.

```
gets (string, string length, file pointer);
```

- The fgets( ) function reads a string from the specified stream until either a new line character or length (– 1) characters have been read. If a new line is read, it will be part of the string. However, fgets( ) is terminated, the resultant string will be null terminated.

		

5. fread() and fwrite() Functions:

- With the help of these command's reading and writing of blocks of data can be done. The standard format is:

Syntax for fread() is:

```
size_tfread (void *buffer, size_tnum_bytes, size_t count, file fp)
```

Syntax for fwrite() is:

```
size_tfwrite (const void *buffer, size_tnum-bytes, size_t count, file *fp);
```

where,

const void buffer is the variable name or array name or structure variable name which is to be written in the file.

size-tnum-bytes is the no. of bytes which the input or output data is expected to occupy. size-t count keeping the above no. of bytes in consideration, the no. of such elements which require above specified memory.

```
file *fp→    file pointer
```

(i) For example:

```
fwrite (& rec1 [i], sizeof (rec1 [0]), 1, fp1)
```

(ii) For example:

```
fwrite (& rec1, size of (rec1 [0]), n, fp1)
```

- The first example (i) tells the compiler to write array element rec1 [1], and the size of it is given by size occupied by rec1 [0]. Only one element is to be written and at last is the file pointer.
- In the second example (ii) we want to write an whole array having n elements in the file. So first we write array name with an ambersand '&' sign, and we have to store 'n' array elements each of size (rec1 [0] i.e. on single array element). So we give size command and at last is the file pointer.

For example:

```
fwrite (&f, sizeof (float), 1, fp)).
```

This declaration of size is also considered as valid. Suppose, we want to write a whole array balance in the file we can write it as,

```
fwrite (balance, sizeof (balance, 1, fp));
```

From the above explanation is quite simple to understand this declaration. As in size we are write, where array, so further we give only '1'.

For fread also all the above declaration holds good, the only difference is we do not have to use the ambersand (&) sign.

For example:

```
fread (balance, size of balance, 1, fp);
```

where balance is an array.

Program 6.9: Program to write a structure element in a file and print it.

```c
#include<stdio.h>
struct record
{
    char customer_name[80];
    int ph_no;
}
customer[10];
void main()
{
    FILE *fp;
    int n,i;
    flushall();
    fp=fopen("input","w");
    clrscr();
    printf("HOW MANY RECORD TO BE FILLED:");
    scanf("%d",&n);
    for(i=0;i<n;i++)
    {
        printf("\nPLEASE ENTER CUSTOMER NAME:");
        scanf("%s", customer[i].customer_name);
        printf("\nPLEASE ENTER PHONE NO.:");
        scanf("%d",&customer[i].ph_no);
        fwrite(&customer[i],sizeof(customer[0]),1,fp);
    }
    fcloseall();
    fp=fopen("input","r");
    printf("\nCUSTOMER NAME \tCUSTOMER PHONE NO.\n");
    for(i=0;i<n;i++)
    {
        fread(&customer[i],sizeof(customer[0]),1,fp);
        printf("\n%s\t%d",customer[i].customer_name,customer[i].ph_no);
    }
    getch();
}
```

Output:

```
How many records to be filled: 2
Please enter customer name: Neelam Enterprises
Please enter ph_no: 628119
Please enter customer name: Modern arts
Please enter ph_no: 661916
            Customer name           Phone no.
    Neelam      enterprises         628119
      Modern          Arts          661916
```

6.6.1 Error Handling Input/Output Operations

- While dealing with files, if some error occurs then it is difficult to detect the error. So we should take care while writing the programs only.
- Typical error situations include:
  (i)   Trying to read beyond the end-of-file mark.
  (ii) Device overflows.
  (iii) Trying to use a file that has not been opened.
  (iv) Trying to perform an operation on a file, when the file is opened for another type of operation.
  (v) Opening a file with invalid filename.
  (vi) Attempting to write to a write-protected file.
- Also to check of success of our command C provides us certain checks.
- We can check the end of file condition by the following command,

```
if(feof (fp))
printf ("end of data")
```

- This feof( ) functions returns a nonzero integer value if all of the data from the specified file has been read, and returns zero otherwise.
- ferror() function determines whether a file operation has produced an error.
- ferror() has following prototype: int ferror(file *fp);
- The ferror function reports the status of the file indicated. It takes FILE pointer as its argument and returns a non-zero integer if an error has been detected upto that point, during processing. It returns zero otherwise.

```
if (ferror (fp) = 0)
printf ("An error has occurred");
```

We can check whether a file is properly opened or not by this command, if (fp = = NULL)

```
printf (" File could not be opened");
```

6.7 PROGRAMS

Program 1: Program to open a file.

```c
#include <stdio.h>
#include <stdlib.h>
int main()
{
    char ch, file_name[25];
    FILE *fp;
    printf("Enter the name of file you wish to see\n");
    gets(file_name);
    fp = fopen(file_name,"r"); //READ  MODE
    if(fp == NULL )
    {
        perror("Error while opening the file.\n");
        exit(EXIT_FAILURE);
    }
```

```c
        printf("The contents of %s file are:\n", file_name);
        while( ( ch = fgetc(fp) ) != EOF )
        printf("%c",ch);
        fclose(fp);
        return 0;
    }
```

Output:

```
Enter the name of file you wish to see
computerprogramming.txt
The contents of computerprogramming.txt file are:
Computer programming is fun.
```

Program 2: Program to copy files.

```c
    #include <stdio.h>
    #include <stdlib.h>
    int main()
    {
        char ch, source_file[20], target_file[20];
        FILE *source, *target;
        printf("Enter name of file to copy\n");
        gets(source_file);
        source = fopen(source_file, "r");
        if( source == NULL )
        {
            printf("Press any key to exit...\n");
            exit(EXIT_FAILURE);
        }
        printf("Enter name of target file\n");
        gets(target_file);
        target = fopen(target_file, "w");
        if( target == NULL )
        {
            fclose(source);
            printf("Press any key to exit...\n");
            exit(EXIT_FAILURE);
        }
        while( ( ch = fgetc(source) ) != EOF )
        fputc(ch, target);
        printf("File copied successfully.\n");
        fclose(source);
        fclose(target);
        return 0;
    }
```

Output:

```
Enter name of file to copy
factorial.c
Enter name of target file
factorial_copy.c
File copied successfully.
```

Program 3: Program to merge files.

```c
#include <stdio.h>
#include <stdlib.h>
int main()
{
    FILE *fs1, *fs2, *ft;
    char ch, file1[20], file2[20], file3[20];
    printf("Enter name of first file\n");
    gets(file1);
    printf("Enter name of second file\n");
    gets(file2);
    printf("Enter name of file which will store contents of two files\n");
    gets(file3);
    fs1 = fopen(file1,"r");
    fs2 = fopen(file2,"r");
    if( fs1 == NULL || fs2 == NULL )
    {
        perror("Error ");
        printf("Press any key to exit...\n");
        getch();
        exit(EXIT_FAILURE);
    }
    ft = fopen(file3,"w");
    if(ft == NULL )
    {
        perror("Error ");
        printf("Press any key to exit...\n");
        exit(EXIT_FAILURE);
    }
    while( ( ch = fgetc(fs1) ) != EOF )
    fputc(ch,ft);
    while( ( ch = fgetc(fs2) ) != EOF )
    fputc(ch,ft);
```

```
        printf("Two files were merged into %s file successfully.\n",file3);
        fclose(fs1);
        fclose(fs2);
        fclose(ft);
        return 0;
    }
```

Output:

```
Enter name of first file
date.c
Enter name of second file
factorial.c
Enter name of file which will store contents of two files date-factorial.c
Two files were merged into date-factorial.c file successfully
```

Program 4: Program to delete a file.

```
#include<stdio.h>
main()
{
    int status;
    char file_name[25];
    printf("Enter the name of file you wish to delete\n");
    gets(file_name);
    status = remove(file_name);
    if( status == 0 )
    printf("%s file deleted successfully.\n",file_name);
    else
    {
        printf("Unable to delete the file\n");
        perror("Error");
    }
    return 0;
}
```

Output:

```
Enter the name of file you wish to delete
leap-year.c
leap-year.c file delete successfully.
```

Program 5: Copy text from one file to other file.

```
#include<stdio.h>
#include<conio.h>
#include<stdlib.h>
```

```c
void main()
{
    FILE *fp1,*fp2;
    char ch;
    clrscr();
    fp1 = fopen("Sample.txt","r");
    fp2 = fopen("Output.txt","w");
    while(1)
    {
        ch = fgetc(fp1);
        if(ch==EOF)
        break;
        else
        putc(ch,fp2);
    }
    printf("File copied succesfully!");
    fclose(fp1);
    fclose(fp2);
}
```

Output:

```
File copied successfully!
```

Explanation: To copy a text from one file to another we have to follow following Steps:

Step 1: Open Source File in Read Mode

 fp1 = fopen("Sample.txt","r");

Step 2: Open Target File in Write Mode

 fp2 = fopen("Output.txt","w");

Step 3: Read Source File Character by Character

```c
    while(1)
     {
     ch = fgetc(fp1);
     if(ch==EOF)
     break;
     else
     putc(ch,fp2);
     }
```

- "fgetc" will read character from source file.
- Check whether character is "End Character of File" or not , if yes then Terminate Loop.
- "putc" will write Single Character on File Pointed by "fp2 pointer.

 Input Text File: C Programming is very funny language

 Output Written on File: C Programming is very funny language.

Program 6: Program for display line by line the contents.

```c
#include<stdio.h>
#include<conio.h>
int main(argc,argv)
intargc;
char *argv[];
{
    FILE *fp;
    charch[100];
    int loop=0;
    if(argc!=2)
    {
        printf("usage is wrong");
        return;
    }
    fp=fopen(argv[1],"r");
    if(fp==NULL)
    {
        printf("file opening error");
        return;
    }
    printf("string\n");
    for(loop=0,ch[loop]=getc(fp);feof(fp)==0;loop++,ch[loop]=getc(fp))
    {
        if(ch[loop]=='\n')
        {
            ch[++loop]='\0';
            printf("%s",ch);
            loop=-1;
        }
    }
    ch[loop]='\0';
    printf("%s",ch);
    fcloseall();
    getch();
}
```

Summary

- A place from where we can reading data or writing data to is File. This includes disk files and it includes devices such as the printer or the monitor of a computer.
- The I/O model does not distinguish between the types of physical devices supporting the I/O. Each source or sink of data (file) is treated in the same way, and is viewed as a stream of bytes.
- A stream is a sequence of bytes of data.
- There are two types of file, text files and binary files, which, within a program, are manipulated as text streams and binary streams once they have been opened for I/O. The stdio package does not permit operations on the contents of files 'directly', but only by viewing them as streams.
- When a program is terminated, the entire data is lost. Storing in a file will preserve your data even if the program terminates.
- File is a collection of information stored in the secondary memory, having some filename, which is stored in the directory.
- Program will consist of accepting character input from user and writing to the file using file processing function 'fputc'.
- With this function we can move the file pointer to a desired position.
- fseek (file ptr, offset, position)
- This function tells where the pointer is positioned right now. It returns this pointer as a long integer which is an offset from the beginning of the file. returns – 1L on error
- long ftell(FILE * fp);
- The fprintf() function outputs the values of the arguments that makes up the argument list as specified in the format string to the stream pointed to by stream. The operations of the format control string and command are identical to those in printf().
- While dealing with files, if some error occurs then it is difficult to detect the error. So we should take care while writing the programs only.

Check Your Understanding

1. When fopen() is not able to open a file, it returns
   - (a) EOF
   - (b) NULL
   - (c) Runtime Error
   - (d) Compiler Dependent
2. getc() returns EOF when
   - (a) End of files is reached
   - (b) When getc() fails to read a character
   - (c) Both of the above
   - (d) None of the above
3. fseek() should be preferred over rewind() mainly because
   - (a) rewind() doesn't work for empty files
   - (b) rewind() may fail for large files
   - (c) In rewind, there is no way to check if the operations completed successfully
   - (d) All of the above

4. What does fp point to in the program?

```
# include &lt; stdio.h &gt;
int main()
{
    File *fp;
    fp = fopen ("trial", "r");
    return 0;
}
```

(a) The first character in the file

(b) The structure which contains a char pointer which points to the first character of a file

(c) The name of the file

(d) The last character in the file

5. Which of the following mode argument is used to truncate?

(a) a   (b) w

(c) f   (d) t

6. FILE is of type ______

(a) int type   (b) char * type

(c) struct type   (d) None of the mentioned

7. For binary files, a ___ must be appended to the mode string.

(a) "b"   (b) "B"

(c) "binary"   (d) "01"

8. It is not possible to combine two or more file opening mode in open () method.

(a) True   (d) False

9. What is the purpose of "rb" in fopen() function used below in the code?

```
    FILE *fp;
fp = fopen("demo.txt", "rb");
```

(a) Open "demo.txt" in binary mode for reading

(b) Create a new file "demo.txt" for reading and writing

(c) Open "demo.txt" in binary mode for reading and writing

(d) None of the above

10. What is the return value of putchar()?

(a) The character written

(b) EOF if an error occurs

(c) Nothing

(d) Both character written & EOF if an error occurs

Answers

1. (b)	2. (c)	3. (c)	4. (b)	5. (b)	6. (c)	7. (a)	8. (d)	9. (a)	10. (d)

Trace the Output

```
1.  main()
    {
        FILE *fP1, *fP2;
        *fP1 = fopen("file.C", "w");
        *fP2 = fopen("file.C", "w");
        fputC('A'), fP1);
        fputC('B'), fP2);
        fclose(fP1);
        fclose(fP2);
    }
2.  main()
    {
        FILE *ptr;
        char i;
        ptr=fopen("myfile.C", "r");
        while((i=fgetc(ptr))! = NULL)
            printf("%c", i);
            return 0;
    }
3.  main()
    {
        FILE *fP;
        char ch, str[7];
        fP=fopen("try.C", "r"); /* file 'try.C' contains "This is Nagpur"  */
        fseek(fP, gL, SEEK_CUR);
        fgets(str, 5, fP);
        puts(str);
        return 0;
    }
```

Practice Questions

Short Answer Questions:

1. What is a file.
2. What is steam?
3. Define text stream and binary stream.
4. What is use of ftell() function.
5. Define fseek() function.

Long Answer Questions:

1. What is the difference between fscanf( ), fprintf( ) and fread( ), fwrite( )?
2. Find out the purpose and use of library functions feof( ).
3. Write a program to remove all blank lines from a file.
4. Explain gets( ) and puts( ) functions.
5. With neat diagram explain following functions:
   (a) rewind( )
   (b) ftell( )
   (c) fseek( )
6. Explain the term fread( ).
7. Explain the term fwrite( ).
8. Explain the term fprintf( ).
9. Explain the term fscanf( ).
10. Explain the term file pointer.
11. With syntax describe following function:
    (a) sscanf( )
    (b) sprintf( )
12. Write C Program that accept file name from user and read data from it if data contains any number or digit replace it with * and display it on terminal.

Previous Exam Questions

Summer 2017

1. Write the purpose of function ftell().

Ans. Refer to Section 6.6.

2. fwrite function writes a block of data from binary file to memory. State true or false.

Ans. Refer to Section 6.5.

3. Explain the file opening modes with their meaning. [3]

Ans. Refer to Section 6.5.

4. What are streams? List the five streams that are automatically opened when runs. [4]

Ans. Refer to Section 6.2.

5. Illustrate how a character can be written to and read from a file. [4]

Ans. Refer to Section 6.5.

Winter 2017

1. What does fp point to in the program?

```c
# include < stdio.h >
int main()
{
    File * fp;
    fp = fopen ("trial", "r");
    return 0;
}
```

    (a) The first character in the file

    (b) The structure which contains a char pointer which points to the first character of a file

    (c) The name of the file

    (d) The last character in the file

2. What is the use of the fseek function.

Ans. Refer to Section 6.6.

3. What are different modes in which file can be opened? [4]

Ans. Refer to Section 6.5.

4. Differentiate between printf and fprintf, scanf and fscanf. [4]

Ans. Refer to Section VI

5. Write the prototype and syntax of the following: [3]

    (i)   fflush( )

    (ii)   remove( )

    (iii) ftell( )

Ans. Refer to Sections 6.6.

Summer 2018

1. Data written into a file using fwrite( ) can be read back using _______ [1]

    (a) fscanf ( )   (b) fread( )

    (c) fgets ( )   (d) All of the above

Ans. (a)

2. Given syntax of fseek( ) function. [1]

Ans. Refer to Section 6.6.

3. Write a C program to copy contents of one file into another file. [4]

Ans. Refer to Section

4. Explain fseek( ) function in detail. [4]

Ans. Refer to Section 6.6.

5. Discuss file opening modes in detail. [4]

Ans. Refer to Section 6.5.

■■■